HOW TO TUTOR WORKBOOK
For
BEGINNING MULTIPLICATION, DIVISION and FRACTIONS

The Paradigm Co., Inc. 3500 Mountain View Dr.   Boise, Idaho 83704
Sept. 2015.   www.alphaphonics@hotmail.com

This workbook was compiled to make your work a little easier.

There are three copies of each page that has problems to be done by the student. The first copy is for your use when explaining and working with your student. The next two copies are for practice. Do not let this workbook limit you. These pages are provided only as an incentive to get started. Feel free to do as Dr. Blumenfeld suggests and make up your own problems [the practice will do you some good].

The timed tests for multiplication and division are based on the rule of thumb that if a pupil knows his tables he/she will be able to have the answer in three seconds. These tests are helpful to build speed but are not to be used to frustrate the student. If the student does not do well the first time encourage him/her that after reviewing he will do better.

**Answers to problems are at the end of each particular section.

Workbook compiled with answer sheets and fraction illustrations done by Barbara J. Simkus.

MULTIPLICATION

Counting by 2's:

2   4   6   8   10   12   14   16   18   20   22   24

Counting by 5's:

5   10   15   20   25   30   35   40   45   50   55   60

Counting by 10's:

10   20   30   40   50   60   70   80   90   100   110   120

Counting by 2's, Fill in the missing number:

2   6   10   14   18   22

     4   8   12   16   20   24

Counting by 5's, Fill in the missing number:

5   15   25   35   45   55

     10   20   30   40   50   60

Counting by 10's, Fill in the missing number:

10   30   50   70   90   110

     20   40   60   80   100   120

Write all by 2's, 5's, and 10's:

MULTIPLICATION FACT TABLE:

EXAMPLE: 2 X 2 = ? Locate the 2 in the top row, then locate the 2 in the outside column, the answer 4 is just below the 2 in the top row.

1	2	3	4	5	6	7	8	9	10	11	12
2	4	6	8	10	12	14	16	18	20	22	24
3	6	9	12	15	18	21	24	27	30	33	36
4	8	12	16	20	24	28	32	36	40	44	48
5	10	15	20	25	30	35	40	45	50	55	60
6	12	18	24	30	36	42	48	54	60	66	72
7	14	21	28	35	42	49	56	63	70	77	84
8	16	24	32	40	48	56	64	72	80	88	96
9	18	27	36	45	54	63	72	81	90	99	108
10	20	30	40	50	60	70	80	90	100	110	120
11	22	33	44	55	66	77	88	99	110	121	132
12	24	36	48	60	72	84	96	108	120	132	144

Multiplication facts - from Pages 245 and 246:

2 x 1 = 2	3 x 1 = 3	4 x 1 = 4	5 x 1 = 5
2 x 2 = 4	3 x 2 = 6	4 x 2 = 8	5 x 2 = 10
2 x 3 = 6	3 x 3 = 9	4 x 3 = 12	5 x 3 = 15
2 x 4 = 8	3 x 4 = 12	4 x 4 = 16	5 x 4 = 20
2 x 5 = 10	3 x 5 = 15	4 x 5 = 20	5 x 5 = 25
2 x 6 = 12	3 x 6 = 18	4 x 6 = 24	5 x 6 = 30
2 x 7 = 14	3 x 7 = 21	4 x 7 = 28	5 x 7 = 35
2 x 8 = 16	3 x 8 = 24	4 x 8 = 32	5 x 8 = 40
2 x 9 = 18	3 x 9 = 27	4 x 9 = 36	5 x 9 = 45

Fill in the answers:

2 x 1 =	3 x 1 =	4 x 1 =	5 x 1 =
2 x 2 =	3 x 2 =	4 x 2 =	5 x 2 =
2 x 3 =	3 x 3 =	4 x 3 =	5 x 3 =
2 x 4 =	3 x 4 =	4 x 4 =	5 x 4 =
2 x 5 =	3 x 5 =	4 x 5 =	5 x 5 =
2 x 6 =	3 x 6 =	4 x 6 =	5 x 6 =
2 x 7 =	3 x 7 =	4 x 7 =	5 x 7 =
2 x 8 =	3 x 8 =	4 x 8 =	5 x 8 =
2 x 9 =	3 x 9 =	4 x 9 =	5 x 9 =

Multiplication Facts - Page 246

6 x 1 = 6	7 x 1 = 7	8 x 1 = 8	9 x 1 = 9	1 x 1 = 1
6 x 2 = 12	7 x 2 = 14	8 x 2 = 16	9 x 2 = 18	1 x 2 = 2
6 x 3 = 18	7 x 3 = 21	8 x 3 = 24	9 x 3 = 27	1 x 3 = 3
6 x 4 = 24	7 x 4 = 28	8 x 4 = 32	9 x 4 = 36	1 x 4 = 4
6 x 5 = 30	7 x 5 = 35	8 x 5 = 40	9 x 5 = 45	1 x 5 = 5
6 x 6 = 36	7 x 6 = 42	8 x 6 = 48	9 x 6 = 54	1 x 6 = 6
6 x 7 = 42	7 x 7 = 49	8 x 7 = 56	9 x 7 = 63	1 x 7 = 7
6 x 8 = 48	7 x 8 = 56	8 x 8 = 64	9 x 8 = 72	1 x 8 = 8
6 x 9 = 54	7 x 9 = 63	8 x 9 = 72	9 x 9 = 81	1 x 9 = 9

Fill in the missing number:

6 x 1 =	7 x 1 =	8 x 1 =	9 x 1 =	1 x 1 =
6 x 2 =	7 x 2 =	8 x 2 =	9 x 2 =	1 x 2 =
6 x 3 =	7 x 3 =	8 x 3 =	9 x 3 =	1 x 3 =
6 x 4 =	7 x 4 =	8 x 4 =	9 x 4 =	1 x 4 =
6 x 5 =	7 x 5 =	8 x 5 =	9 x 5 =	1 x 5 =
6 x 6 =	7 x 6 =	8 x 6 =	9 x 6 =	1 x 6 =
6 x 7 =	7 x 7 =	8 x 7 =	9 x 7 =	1 x 7 =
6 x 8 =	7 x 8 =	8 x 8 =	9 x 8 =	1 x 8 =
6 x 9 =	7 x 9 =	8 x 9 =	9 x 9 =	1 x 9 =

Multiplication facts – Practice

2 x 1 =	3 x 1 =	4 x 1 =	5 x 1 =
2 x 2 =	3 x 2 =	4 x 2 =	5 x 2 =
2 x 3 =	3 x 3 =	4 x 3 =	5 x 3 =
2 x 4 =	3 x 4 =	4 x 4 =	5 x 4 =
2 x 5 =	3 x 5 =	4 x 5 =	5 x 5 =
2 x 6 =	3 x 6 =	4 x 6 =	5 x 6 =
2 x 7 =	3 x 7 =	4 x 7 =	5 x 7 =
2 x 8 =	3 x 8 =	4 x 8 =	5 x 8 =
2 x 9 =	3 x 9 =	4 x 9 =	5 x 9 =

6 x 1 =	7 x 1 =	8 x 1 =	9 x 1 =	1 x 1 =
6 x 2 =	7 x 2 =	8 x 2 =	9 x 2 =	1 x 2 =
6 x 3 =	7 x 3 =	8 x 3 =	9 x 3 =	1 x 3 =
6 x 4 =	7 x 4 =	8 x 4 =	9 x 4 =	1 x 4 =
6 x 5 =	7 x 5 =	8 x 5 =	9 x 5 =	1 x 5 =
6 x 6 =	7 x 6 =	8 x 6 =	9 x 6 =	1 x 6 =
6 x 7 =	7 x 7 =	8 x 7 =	9 x 7 =	1 x 7 =
6 x 8 =	7 x 8 =	8 x 8 =	9 x 8 =	1 x 8 =
6 x 9 =	7 x 9 =	8 x 9 =	9 x 9 =	1 x 9 =

Multiplication facts – Practice

2 x 1 =	3 x 1 =	4 x 1 =	5 x 1 =
2 x 2 =	3 x 2 =	4 x 2 =	5 x 2 =
2 x 3 =	3 x 3 =	4 x 3 =	5 x 3 =
2 x 4 =	3 x 4 =	4 x 4 =	5 x 4 =
2 x 5 =	3 x 5 =	4 x 5 =	5 x 5 =
2 x 6 =	3 x 6 =	4 x 6 =	5 x 6 =
2 x 7 =	3 x 7 =	4 x 7 =	5 x 7 =
2 x 8 =	3 x 8 =	4 x 8 =	5 x 8 =
2 x 9 =	3 x 9 =	4 x 9 =	5 x 9 =

6 x 1 =	7 x 1 =	8 x 1 =	9 x 1 =	1 x 1 =
6 x 2 =	7 x 2 =	8 x 2 =	9 x 2 =	1 x 2 =
6 x 3 =	7 x 3 =	8 x 3 =	9 x 3 =	1 x 3 =
6 x 4 =	7 x 4 =	8 x 4 =	9 x 4 =	1 x 4 =
6 x 5 =	7 x 5 =	8 x 5 =	9 x 5 =	1 x 5 =
6 x 6 =	7 x 6 =	8 x 6 =	9 x 6 =	1 x 6 =
6 x 7 =	7 x 7 =	8 x 7 =	9 x 7 =	1 x 7 =
6 x 8 =	7 x 8 =	8 x 8 =	9 x 8 =	1 x 8 =
6 x 9 =	7 x 9 =	8 x 9 =	9 x 9 =	1 x 9 =

Multiplication facts – Practice

2 x 1 =	3 x 1 =	4 x 1 =	5 x 1 =
2 x 2 =	3 x 2 =	4 x 2 =	5 x 2 =
2 x 3 =	3 x 3 =	4 x 3 =	5 x 3 =
2 x 4 =	3 x 4 =	4 x 4 =	5 x 4 =
2 x 5 =	3 x 5 =	4 x 5 =	5 x 5 =
2 x 6 =	3 x 6 =	4 x 6 =	5 x 6 =
2 x 7 =	3 x 7 =	4 x 7 =	5 x 7 =
2 x 8 =	3 x 8 =	4 x 8 =	5 x 8 =
2 x 9 =	3 x 9 =	4 x 9 =	5 x 9 =

6 x 1 =	7 x 1 =	8 x 1 =	9 x 1 =	1 x 1 =
6 x 2 =	7 x 2 =	8 x 2 =	9 x 2 =	1 x 2 =
6 x 3 =	7 x 3 =	8 x 3 =	9 x 3 =	1 x 3 =
6 x 4 =	7 x 4 =	8 x 4 =	9 x 4 =	1 x 4 =
6 x 5 =	7 x 5 =	8 x 5 =	9 x 5 =	1 x 5 =
6 x 6 =	7 x 6 =	8 x 6 =	9 x 6 =	1 x 6 =
6 x 7 =	7 x 7 =	8 x 7 =	9 x 7 =	1 x 7 =
6 x 8 =	7 x 8 =	8 x 8 =	9 x 8 =	1 x 8 =
6 x 9 =	7 x 9 =	8 x 9 =	9 x 9 =	1 x 9 =

MULTIPLICATION EXERCISES PAGE 249.

1 x2 2	2 x2 4	3 x2 6	4 x2 8	5 x2 10	6 x2 12	7 x2 14	8 x2 16	9 x2 18
1 x3 3	2 x3 6	3 x3 9	4 x3 12	5 x3 15	6 x3 18	7 x3 21	8 x3 24	9 x3 27
1 x4 4	2 x4 8	3 x4 12	4 x4 16	5 x4 20	6 x4 24	7 x4 28	8 x4 32	9 x4 36
1 x5 5	2 x5 10	3 x5 15	4 x5 20	5 x5 25	6 x5 30	7 x5 35	8 x5 40	9 x5 45
1 x6 6	2 x6 12	3 x6 18	4 x6 24	5 x6 30	6 x6 36	7 x6 42	8 x6 48	9 x6 54
1 x7 7	2 x7 14	3 x7 21	4 x7 28	5 x7 35	6 x7 42	7 x7 49	8 x7 56	9 x7 63
1 x8 8	2 x8 16	3 x8 24	4 x8 32	5 x8 40	6 x8 48	7 x8 56	8 x8 64	9 x8 72
1 x9 9	2 x9 18	3 x9 27	4 x9 36	5 x9 45	6 x9 54	7 x9 63	8 x9 72	9 x9 81

MULTIPLICATION EXERCISES PAGE 249.

1	2	3	4	5	6	7	8	9
x2	x2	x2	x2	x2	x2	x2	x2	x2

1	2	3	4	5	6	7	8	9
x3	x3	x3	x3	x3	x3	x3	x3	x3

1	2	3	4	5	6	7	8	9
x4	x4	x4	x4	x4	x4	x4	x4	x4

1	2	3	4	5	6	7	8	9
x5	x5	x5	x5	x5	x5	x5	x5	x5

1	2	3	4	5	6	7	8	9
x6	x6	x6	x6	x6	x6	x6	x6	x6

1	2	3	4	5	6	7	8	9
x7	x7	x7	x7	x7	x7	x7	x7	x7

1	2	3	4	5	6	7	8	9
x8	x8	x8	x8	x8	x8	x8	x8	x8

1	2	3	4	5	6	7	8	9
x9	x9	x9	x9	x9	x9	x9	x9	x9

MULTIPLICATION EXERCISES PAGE 249.

1	2	3	4	5	6	7	8	9
x2	x2	x2	x2	x2	x2	x2	x2	x2

1	2	3	4	5	6	7	8	9
x3	x3	x3	x3	x3	x3	x3	x3	x3

1	2	3	4	5	6	7	8	9
x4	x4	x4	x4	x4	x4	x4	x4	x4

1	2	3	4	5	6	7	8	9
x5	x5	x5	x5	x5	x5	x5	x5	x5

1	2	3	4	5	6	7	8	9
x6	x6	x6	x6	x6	x6	x6	x6	x6

1	2	3	4	5	6	7	8	9
x7	x7	x7	x7	x7	x7	x7	x7	x7

1	2	3	4	5	6	7	8	9
x8	x8	x8	x8	x8	x8	x8	x8	x8

1	2	3	4	5	6	7	8	9
x9	x9	x9	x9	x9	x9	x9	x9	x9

MULTIPLICATION EXERCISES PAGE 249.

1	2	3	4	5	6	7	8	9
x2	x2	x2	x2	x2	x2	x2	x2	x2

1	2	3	4	5	6	7	8	9
x3	x3	x3	x3	x3	x3	x3	x3	x3

1	2	3	4	5	6	7	8	9
x4	x4	x4	x4	x4	x4	x4	x4	x4

1	2	3	4	5	6	7	8	9
x5	x5	x5	x5	x5	x5	x5	x5	x5

1	2	3	4	5	6	7	8	9
x6	x6	x6	x6	x6	x6	x6	x6	x6

1	2	3	4	5	6	7	8	9
x7	x7	x7	x7	x7	x7	x7	x7	x7

1	2	3	4	5	6	7	8	9
x8	x8	x8	x8	x8	x8	x8	x8	x8

1	2	3	4	5	6	7	8	9
x9	x9	x9	x9	x9	x9	x9	x9	x9

More Practice in counting.

By 3's:

3 6 9 12 15 18 21 24 27 30 33 36

By 4's:

4 8 12 16 20 24 28 32 36 40 44 48

By 6's:

6 12 18 24 30 36 42 48 54 60 66 72

By 7's:

7 14 21 28 35 42 49 56 63 70 77 84

By 8's:

8 16 24 32 40 48 56 64 72 80 88 96

By 9's:

9 18 27 36 45 54 63 72 81 90 99 108

By 11's:

11 22 33 44 55 66 77 88 99 110 121 132

By 12's:

12 24 36 48 60 72 84 96 108 120 132 144

Multiples of 15 are very common and recur often in math.
15's:

15 30 45 60 75 90 105 120 135 150 165 180

EXERCISES FOR PAGE 250 and PAGE 251:

```
 5  Multiplicand
X2  Multiplier
10  Product
```

11	21	31	41	51	61	71	81	91	12
x2	x2	x2	x2	x2	x2	x2	x2	x2	x2

22	32	42	52	62	72	82	92	13	23
x2	x2	x2	x2	x2	x2	x2	x2	x2	x2

33	43	53	63	73	83	93	14	24	34
x2	x2	x2	x2	x2	x2	x2	x2	x2	x2

44	54	64	74	84	94	40	50	60	70
x2	x2	x2	x2	x2	x2	x2	x2	x2	x2

80	90	21	81	42	91	41	81	63	61
x2	x2	x5	x7	x4	x8	x6	x9	x3	x7

EXERCISES FOR PAGE 250 and PAGE 251:

```
 5  Multiplicand
X2  Multiplier
10  Product
```

11	21	31	41	51	61	71	81	91	12
x2	x2	x2	x2	x2	x2	x2	x2	x2	x2

22	32	42	52	62	72	82	92	13	23
x2	x2	x2	x2	x2	x2	x2	x2	x2	x2

33	43	53	63	73	83	93	14	24	34
x2	x2	x2	x2	x2	x2	x2	x2	x2	x2

44	54	64	74	84	94	40	50	60	70
x2	x2	x2	x2	x2	x2	x2	x2	x2	x2

80	90	21	81	42	91	41	81	63	61
x2	x2	x5	x7	x4	x8	x6	x9	x3	x7

EXERCISES FOR PAGE 250 and PAGE 251:

```
 5  Multiplicand
X2  Multiplier
10  Product
```

11	21	31	41	51	61	71	81	91	12
x2	x2	x2	x2	x2	x2	x2	x2	x2	x2

22	32	42	52	62	72	82	92	13	23
x2	x2	x2	x2	x2	x2	x2	x2	x2	x2

33	43	53	63	73	83	93	14	24	34
x2	x2	x2	x2	x2	x2	x2	x2	x2	x2

44	54	64	74	84	94	40	50	60	70
x2	x2	x2	x2	x2	x2	x2	x2	x2	x2

80	90	21	81	42	91	41	81	63	61
x2	x2	x5	x7	x4	x8	x6	x9	x3	x7

EXERCISES FROM PAGE 251:

```
 51    72    51    72    61    81    51    62    41    83
 x5    x4    x8    x3    x9    x6    x7    x4    x5    x2

 71    61    71    41    81    41    92    71    61    71
 x8    x6    x9    x7    x8    x9    x2    x4    x8    x7

 30    52    60    80    40    52    90    90    30    20
 x9    x4    x2    x5    x8    x2    x7    x3    x7    x8

 82    30    90    90    42    50    51    90    30    70
 x3    x6    x5    x9    x3    x9    x6    x4    x5    x6

 31    32    91    21    20    21    52    61    71    82
 x8    x4    x6    x9    x7    x6    x3    x5    x5    x4

 82    70    20    71    83    61    70    34    23    12
 x4    x6    x8    x7    x2    x7    x2    x2    x2    x2

 63    41    61    30    30    71    61    90    90    71
 x3    x5    x8    x7    x5    x5    x5    x4    x3    x4

 62    81    41    51    92    90    51    52    21    50
 x4    x4    x3    x6    x2    x7    x6    x3    x6    x9

 80    51    71    30    82    31    32    30    52    61
 x2    x5    x8    x9    x3    x8    x4    x6    x4    x6
```

EXERCISES FROM PAGE 251:

51	72	51	72	61	81	51	62	41	83
x5	x4	x8	x3	x9	x6	x7	x4	x5	x2

71	61	71	41	81	41	92	71	61	71
x8	x6	x9	x7	x8	x9	x2	x4	x8	x7

30	52	60	80	40	52	90	90	30	20
x9	x4	x2	x5	x8	x2	x7	x3	x7	x8

82	30	90	90	42	50	51	90	30	70
x3	x6	x5	x9	x3	x9	x6	x4	x5	x6

31	32	91	21	20	21	52	61	71	82
x8	x4	x6	x9	x7	x6	x3	x5	x5	x4

82	70	20	71	83	61	70	34	23	12
x4	x6	x8	x7	x2	x7	x2	x2	x2	x2

63	41	61	30	30	71	61	90	90	71
x3	x5	x8	x7	x5	x5	x5	x4	x3	x4

62	81	41	51	92	90	51	52	21	50
x4	x4	x3	x6	x2	x7	x6	x3	x6	x9

80	51	71	30	82	31	32	30	52	61
x2	x5	x8	x9	x3	x8	x4	x6	x4	x6

EXERCISES FROM PAGE 251:

51	72	51	72	61	81	51	62	41	83
x5	x4	x8	x3	x9	x6	x7	x4	x5	x2
71	61	71	41	81	41	92	71	61	71
x8	x6	x9	x7	x8	x9	x2	x4	x8	x7
30	52	60	80	40	52	90	90	30	20
x9	x4	x2	x5	x8	x2	x7	x3	x7	x8
82	30	90	90	42	50	51	90	30	70
x3	x6	x5	x9	x3	x9	x6	x4	x5	x6
31	32	91	21	20	21	52	61	71	82
x8	x4	x6	x9	x7	x6	x3	x5	x5	x4
82	70	20	71	83	61	70	34	23	12
x4	x6	x8	x7	x2	x7	x2	x2	x2	x2
63	41	61	30	30	71	61	90	90	71
x3	x5	x8	x7	x5	x5	x5	x4	x3	x4
62	81	41	51	92	90	51	52	21	50
x4	x4	x3	x6	x2	x7	x6	x3	x6	x9
80	51	71	30	82	31	32	30	52	61
x2	x5	x8	x9	x3	x8	x4	x6	x4	x6

TIMED TEST FOR MULTIPLICATION FACTS:

[4 MIN. 5 SEC.]

$2 \times 1 =$	$3 \times 1 =$	$4 \times 1 =$	$5 \times 1 =$
$2 \times 2 =$	$3 \times 2 =$	$4 \times 2 =$	$5 \times 2 =$
$2 \times 3 =$	$3 \times 3 =$	$4 \times 3 =$	$5 \times 3 =$
$2 \times 4 =$	$3 \times 4 =$	$4 \times 4 =$	$5 \times 4 =$
$2 \times 5 =$	$3 \times 5 =$	$4 \times 5 =$	$5 \times 5 =$
$2 \times 6 =$	$3 \times 6 =$	$4 \times 6 =$	$5 \times 6 =$
$2 \times 7 =$	$3 \times 7 =$	$4 \times 7 =$	$5 \times 7 =$
$2 \times 8 =$	$3 \times 8 =$	$4 \times 8 =$	$5 \times 8 =$
$2 \times 9 =$	$3 \times 9 =$	$4 \times 9 =$	$5 \times 9 =$

$6 \times 1 =$	$7 \times 1 =$	$8 \times 1 =$	$9 \times 1 =$	$1 \times 1 =$
$6 \times 2 =$	$7 \times 2 =$	$8 \times 2 =$	$9 \times 2 =$	$1 \times 2 =$
$6 \times 3 =$	$7 \times 3 =$	$8 \times 3 =$	$9 \times 3 =$	$1 \times 3 =$
$6 \times 4 =$	$7 \times 4 =$	$8 \times 4 =$	$9 \times 4 =$	$1 \times 4 =$
$6 \times 5 =$	$7 \times 5 =$	$8 \times 5 =$	$9 \times 5 =$	$1 \times 5 =$
$6 \times 6 =$	$7 \times 6 =$	$8 \times 6 =$	$9 \times 6 =$	$1 \times 6 =$
$6 \times 7 =$	$7 \times 7 =$	$8 \times 7 =$	$9 \times 7 =$	$1 \times 7 =$
$6 \times 8 =$	$7 \times 8 =$	$8 \times 8 =$	$9 \times 8 =$	$1 \times 8 =$
$6 \times 9 =$	$7 \times 9 =$	$8 \times 9 =$	$9 \times 9 =$	$1 \times 9 =$

Over:
19a
(Blank for practice)

TIMED TEST FOR MULTIPLICATION FACTS:

[4 MIN. 5 SEC.]

2 x 1 =	3 x 1 =	4 x 1 =	5 x 1 =
2 x 2 =	3 x 2 =	4 x 2 =	5 x 2 =
2 x 3 =	3 x 3 =	4 x 3 =	5 x 3 =
2 x 4 =	3 x 4 =	4 x 4 =	5 x 4 =
2 x 5 =	3 x 5 =	4 x 5 =	5 x 5 =
2 x 6 =	3 x 6 =	4 x 6 =	5 x 6 =
2 x 7 =	3 x 7 =	4 x 7 =	5 x 7 =
2 x 8 =	3 x 8 =	4 x 8 =	5 x 8 =
2 x 9 =	3 x 9 =	4 x 9 =	5 x 9 =

6 x 1 =	7 x 1 =	8 x 1 =	9 x 1 =	1 x 1 =
6 x 2 =	7 x 2 =	8 x 2 =	9 x 2 =	1 x 2 =
6 x 3 =	7 x 3 =	8 x 3 =	9 x 3 =	1 x 3 =
6 x 4 =	7 x 4 =	8 x 4 =	9 x 4 =	1 x 4 =
6 x 5 =	7 x 5 =	8 x 5 =	9 x 5 =	1 x 5 =
6 x 6 =	7 x 6 =	8 x 6 =	9 x 6 =	1 x 6 =
6 x 7 =	7 x 7 =	8 x 7 =	9 x 7 =	1 x 7 =
6 x 8 =	7 x 8 =	8 x 8 =	9 x 8 =	1 x 8 =
6 x 9 =	7 x 9 =	8 x 9 =	9 x 9 =	1 x 9 =

Over:
20a
(Blank for practice)

[4 MIN. 5 SEC.]

2 x 1 =	3 x 1 =	4 x 1 =	5 x 1 =
2 x 2 =	3 x 2 =	4 x 2 =	5 x 2 =
2 x 3 =	3 x 3 =	4 x 3 =	5 x 3 =
2 x 4 =	3 x 4 =	4 x 4 =	5 x 4 =
2 x 5 =	3 x 5 =	4 x 5 =	5 x 5 =
2 x 6 =	3 x 6 =	4 x 6 =	5 x 6 =
2 x 7 =	3 x 7 =	4 x 7 =	5 x 7 =
2 x 8 =	3 x 8 =	4 x 8 =	5 x 8 =
2 x 9 =	3 x 9 =	4 x 9 =	5 x 9 =

6 x 1 =	7 x 1 =	8 x 1 =	9 x 1 =	1 x 1 =
6 x 2 =	7 x 2 =	8 x 2 =	9 x 2 =	1 x 2 =
6 x 3 =	7 x 3 =	8 x 3 =	9 x 3 =	1 x 3 =
6 x 4 =	7 x 4 =	8 x 4 =	9 x 4 =	1 x 4 =
6 x 5 =	7 x 5 =	8 x 5 =	9 x 5 =	1 x 5 =
6 x 6 =	7 x 6 =	8 x 6 =	9 x 6 =	1 x 6 =
6 x 7 =	7 x 7 =	8 x 7 =	9 x 7 =	1 x 7 =
6 x 8 =	7 x 8 =	8 x 8 =	9 x 8 =	1 x 8 =
6 x 9 =	7 x 9 =	8 x 9 =	9 x 9 =	1 x 9 =

Over:
21a
(Blank for practice)

TIMED TEST FOR MULTIPLICATION FACTS MIXED
[TIME 3 MIN. 45 SEC.]

4 x2	6 x3	3 x5	8 x7	9 x2	7 x4	5 x6	2 x2
1 x9	5 x8	7 x7	1 x3	4 x5	9 x4	3 x3	6 x6
8 x2	2 x9	9 x7	5 x4	3 x8	1 x6	4 x8	7 x3
2 x6	6 x9	8 x3	1 x5	2 x7	3 x7	4 x9	5 x5
6 x8	7 x8	8 x5	9 x9	8 x9	6 x5	4 x4	3 x9
1 x8	2 x3	5 x9	7 x6	9 x3	2 x5	4 x7	6 x2
8 x8	1 x7	3 x6	5 x7	7 x9	9 x6	1 x4	3 x2
5 x3	7 x5	9 x8	2 x4	4 x6	6 x7	8 x4	9 x5
8 x6	7 x2	6 x4	5 x2	4 x3	3 x4	2 x8	1 x2

TIMED TEST FOR MULTIPLICATION FACTS MIXED
[TIME 3 MIN. 45 SEC.]

4	6	3	8	9	7	5	2
x2	x3	x5	x7	x2	x4	x6	x2

1	5	7	1	4	9	3	6
x9	x8	x7	x3	x5	x4	x3	x6

8	2	9	5	3	1	4	7
x2	x9	x7	x4	x8	x6	x8	x3

2	6	8	1	2	3	4	5
x6	x9	x3	x5	x7	x7	x9	x5

6	7	8	9	8	6	4	3
x8	x8	x5	x9	x9	x5	x4	x9

1	2	5	7	9	2	4	6
x8	x3	x9	x6	x3	x5	x7	x2

8	1	3	5	7	9	1	3
x8	x7	x6	x7	x9	x6	x4	x2

5	7	9	2	4	6	8	9
x3	x5	x8	x4	x6	x7	x4	x5

8	7	6	5	4	3	2	1
x6	x2	x4	x2	x3	x4	x8	x2

Over:
23a
(Blank for practice)

TIMED TEST FOR MULTIPLICATION FACTS MIXED
[TIME 3 MIN. 45 SEC.]

4 x2	6 x3	3 x5	8 x7	9 x2	7 x4	5 x6	2 x2
1 x9	5 x8	7 x7	1 x3	4 x5	9 x4	3 x3	6 x6
8 x2	2 x9	9 x7	5 x4	3 x8	1 x6	4 x8	7 x3
2 x6	6 x9	8 x3	1 x5	2 x7	3 x7	4 x9	5 x5
6 x8	7 x8	8 x5	9 x9	8 x9	6 x5	4 x4	3 x9
1 x8	2 x3	5 x9	7 x6	9 x3	2 x5	4 x7	6 x2
8 x8	1 x7	3 x6	5 x7	7 x9	9 x6	1 x4	3 x2
5 x3	7 x5	9 x8	2 x4	4 x6	6 x7	8 x4	9 x5
8 x6	7 x2	6 x4	5 x2	4 x3	3 x4	2 x8	1 x2

**Over:
24a
(Blank for practice)**

EXERCISES PAGE 252:

```
1.   15      2.   ²15      3.   ²15
     x5           x5            x5
                   5           75
```

```
 65     46     57     79     63     32     84     45     35
 x2     x3     x5     x2     x4     x6     x2     x4     x3
```

```
 43     32     22     26     27     25     22     43     26
 x5     x2     x8     x3     x5     x7     x9     x6     x4
```

```
 28     46     47     53     52     96     74     28     53
 x3     x4     x2     x5     x4     x2     x3     x5     x8
```

```
 45     35     49     28     54     35     37     23     96
 x6     x3     x5     x2     x7     x9     x4     x7     x3
```

```
 67     42     89     24     37     29     28     19     62
 x5     x9     x4     x8     x4     x7     x5     x3     x8
```

```
 46     35     27     62     38     62     46     17     37
 x2     x9     x3     x4     x2     x9     x6     x8     x5
```

EXERCISES PAGE 252:

1. 15
     x5

2. $\overset{2}{15}$
     x5
      5

3. $\overset{2}{15}$
     x5
     75

65	46	57	79	63	32	84	45	35
x2	x3	x5	x2	x4	x6	x2	x4	x3

43	32	22	26	27	25	22	43	26
x5	x2	x8	x3	x5	x7	x9	x6	x4

28	46	47	53	52	96	74	28	53
x3	x4	x2	x5	x4	x2	x3	x5	x8

45	35	49	28	54	35	37	23	96
x6	x3	x5	x2	x7	x9	x4	x7	x3

67	42	89	24	37	29	28	19	62
x5	x9	x4	x8	x4	x7	x5	x3	x8

46	35	27	62	38	62	46	17	37
x2	x9	x3	x4	x2	x9	x6	x8	x5

EXERCISES PAGE 252:

1. 15
    x5

2. $\overset{2}{15}$
    x5
    5

3. $\overset{2}{15}$
    x5
    75

| 65 | 46 | 57 | 79 | 63 | 32 | 84 | 45 | 35 |
| x2 | x3 | x5 | x2 | x4 | x6 | x2 | x4 | x3 |

| 43 | 32 | 22 | 26 | 27 | 25 | 22 | 43 | 26 |
| x5 | x2 | x8 | x3 | x5 | x7 | x9 | x6 | x4 |

| 28 | 46 | 47 | 53 | 52 | 96 | 74 | 28 | 53 |
| x3 | x4 | x2 | x5 | x4 | x2 | x3 | x5 | x8 |

| 45 | 35 | 49 | 28 | 54 | 35 | 37 | 23 | 96 |
| x6 | x3 | x5 | x2 | x7 | x9 | x4 | x7 | x3 |

| 67 | 42 | 89 | 24 | 37 | 29 | 28 | 19 | 62 |
| x5 | x9 | x4 | x8 | x4 | x7 | x5 | x3 | x8 |

| 46 | 35 | 27 | 62 | 38 | 62 | 46 | 17 | 37 |
| x2 | x9 | x3 | x4 | x2 | x9 | x6 | x8 | x5 |

EXERCISES PAGE 253:

Multiplication with carrying.

35 x8	18 x4	49 x5	68 x7	59 x6	84 x3	74 x9	57 x2	87 x6
16 x5	84 x8	49 x4	91 x9	35 x3	19 x2	37 x7	57 x7	59 x4
98 x9	72 x6	69 x3	95 x5	79 x8	84 x8	68 x6	48 x3	97 x9
79 x7	74 x4	86 x7	79 x6	48 x9	69 x8	93 x3	98 x4	34 x7
73 x8	36 x9	43 x6	63 x4	76 x3	43 x3	39 x8	93 x7	67 x6
74 x7	97 x3	98 x6	73 x4	43 x6	48 x8	73 x9	48 x9	76 x8
87 x6	59 x4	97 x9	34 x7	67 x6	76 x8	48 x9	93 x7	68 x4
35 x3	26 x4	53 x8	96 x3	62 x8	37 x5	17 x8	19 x3	23 x7

EXERCISES PAGE 253:

Multiplication with carrying.

35	18	49	68	59	84	74	57	87
x8	x4	x5	x7	x6	x3	x9	x2	x6

16	84	49	91	35	19	37	57	59
x5	x8	x4	x9	x3	x2	x7	x7	x4

98	72	69	95	79	84	68	48	97
x9	x6	x3	x5	x8	x8	x6	x3	x9

79	74	86	79	48	69	93	98	34
x7	x4	x7	x6	x9	x8	x3	x4	x7

73	36	43	63	76	43	39	93	67
x8	x9	x6	x4	x3	x3	x8	x7	x6

74	97	98	73	43	48	73	48	76
x7	x3	x6	x4	x6	x8	x9	x9	x8

87	59	97	34	67	76	48	93	68
x6	x4	x9	x7	x6	x8	x9	x7	x4

35	26	53	96	62	37	17	19	23
x3	x4	x8	x3	x8	x5	x8	x3	x7

EXERCISES PAGE 253:

Multiplication with carrying.

35	18	49	68	59	84	74	57	87
x8	x4	x5	x7	x6	x3	x9	x2	x6

16	84	49	91	35	19	37	57	59
x5	x8	x4	x9	x3	x2	x7	x7	x4

98	72	69	95	79	84	68	48	97
x9	x6	x3	x5	x8	x8	x6	x3	x9

79	74	86	79	48	69	93	98	34
x7	x4	x7	x6	x9	x8	x3	x4	x7

73	36	43	63	76	43	39	93	67
x8	x9	x6	x4	x3	x3	x8	x7	x6

74	97	98	73	43	48	73	48	76
x7	x3	x6	x4	x6	x8	x9	x9	x8

87	59	97	34	67	76	48	93	68
x6	x4	x9	x7	x6	x8	x9	x7	x4

35	26	53	96	62	37	17	19	23
x3	x4	x8	x3	x8	x5	x8	x3	x7

ANSWERS

Answers for Timed Test Multiplication Mixed:

Row 1: 8, 18, 15, 56, 18, 28, 30, 4

Row 2: 9, 40, 49, 3, 20, 36, 9, 36

Row 3: 16, 18, 63, 20, 24, 6, 32, 21

Row 4: 12, 54, 24, 5, 14, 21, 36, 25

Row 5: 48, 56, 40, 81, 72, 30, 16, 27

Row 6: 8, 6, 45, 42, 27, 10, 28, 12

Row 7: 64, 7, 18, 35, 63, 54, 4, 6

Row 8: 15, 35, 72, 8, 24, 42, 32, 45

Row 9: 48, 14, 24, 10, 12, 12, 16, 2

MULTIPLICATION ANSWERS

ANSWERS FOR PAGE LABELED PAGES 250 AND 251:

Row 1: 22, 42, 62, 82, 102, 122, 142, 162, 192, 24
Row 2: 44, 64, 84, 104, 124, 144, 164, 184, 26, 46
Row 3: 66, 86, 106, 126, 146, 166, 186, 28, 48, 68
Row 4: 88, 108, 128, 148, 168, 188, 80, 100, 120, 140
Row 5: 160, 180, 105, 567, 168, 728, 246, 729, 189, 427

ANSWERS TO PROBLEMS PAGE LABELED 251:
Row 1: 255, 288, 408, 216, 549, 486, 357, 248, 205, 166
Row 2: 568, 366, 639, 287, 648, 369, 184, 284, 488, 497
Row 3: 270, 208, 120, 400, 328, 104, 630, 270, 210, 160
Row 4: 246, 180, 400, 810, 126, 450, 306, 360, 150, 420
Row 5: 248, 128, 546, 189, 140, 126, 156, 305, 355, 328
Row 6: 328, 420, 160, 497, 166, 427, 140, 66, 46, 24
Row 7: 189, 205, 488, 210, 150, 355, 305, 360, 270, 284
Row 8: 248, 324, 123, 306, 184, 630, 306, 156, 126, 450
Row 9: 160, 255, 568, 270, 246, 248, 128, 180, 208, 366

ANSWERS TO PROBLEMS ON PAGE LABELED 252:

Row 1: 130, 138, 285, 158, 252, 192, 168, 180, 105
Row 2: 215, 64, 176, 78, 135, 175, 198, 258, 104
Row 3: 84, 184, 94, 265, 208, 192, 222, 140, 424
Row 4: 270, 105, 245, 56, 378, 315, 148, 161, 288
Row 5: 335, 378, 356, 192, 148, 203, 140, 57, 496
Row 6: 92, 315, 81, 248, 76, 558, 276, 136, 185

ANSWERS TO PROBLEMS ON PAGE LABELED 253:

Row 1: 280, 72, 245, 476, 354, 252, 666, 114, 522
Row 2: 80, 672, 196, 819, 105, 38, 259, 399, 236
Row 3: 882, 432, 207, 475, 632, 672, 408, 144, 873
Row 4: 553, 296, 602, 474, 432, 552, 279, 392, 238
Row 5: 584, 324, 258, 252, 228, 129, 312, 651, 402
Row 6: 518, 291, 588, 292, 258, 384, 657, 432, 608
Row 7: 522, 236, 873, 238, 402, 608, 432, 651, 272
Row 8: 105, 104, 424, 288, 496, 185, 136, 57, 161

DIVISION ÷ DIVISION

DIVISION FACTS — Pages 254 and 255

$2 \times 1 = 2$	$2 \div 2 = 1$	$3 \times 1 = 3$	$3 \div 3 = 1$
$2 \times 2 = 4$	$4 \div 2 = 2$	$3 \times 2 = 6$	$6 \div 3 = 2$
$2 \times 3 = 6$	$6 \div 2 = 3$	$3 \times 3 = 9$	$9 \div 3 = 3$
$2 \times 4 = 8$	$8 \div 2 = 4$	$3 \times 4 = 12$	$12 \div 3 = 4$
$2 \times 5 = 10$	$10 \div 2 = 5$	$3 \times 5 = 15$	$15 \div 3 = 5$
$2 \times 6 = 12$	$12 \div 2 = 6$	$3 \times 6 = 18$	$18 \div 3 = 6$
$2 \times 7 = 14$	$14 \div 2 = 7$	$3 \times 7 = 21$	$21 \div 3 = 7$
$2 \times 8 = 16$	$16 \div 2 = 8$	$3 \times 8 = 24$	$24 \div 3 = 8$
$2 \times 9 = 18$	$18 \div 2 = 9$	$3 \times 9 = 27$	$27 \div 3 = 9$
$4 \times 1 = 4$	$4 \div 4 = 1$	$5 \times 1 = 5$	$5 \div 5 = 1$
$4 \times 2 = 8$	$8 \div 4 = 2$	$5 \times 2 = 10$	$10 \div 5 = 2$
$4 \times 3 = 12$	$12 \div 4 = 3$	$5 \times 3 = 15$	$15 \div 5 = 3$
$4 \times 4 = 16$	$16 \div 4 = 4$	$5 \times 4 = 20$	$20 \div 5 = 4$
$4 \times 5 = 20$	$20 \div 4 = 5$	$5 \times 5 = 25$	$25 \div 5 = 5$
$4 \times 6 = 24$	$24 \div 4 = 6$	$5 \times 6 = 30$	$30 \div 5 = 6$
$4 \times 7 = 28$	$28 \div 4 = 7$	$5 \times 7 = 35$	$35 \div 5 = 7$
$4 \times 8 = 32$	$32 \div 4 = 8$	$5 \times 8 = 40$	$40 \div 5 = 8$
$4 \times 9 = 36$	$36 \div 4 = 9$	$5 \times 9 = 45$	$45 \div 5 = 9$

DIVISION FACTS — Pages 255 and 256.

6 x 1 = 6	6 ÷ 6 = 1	7 x 1 = 7	7 ÷ 7 = 1
6 x 2 = 12	12 ÷ 6 = 2	7 x 2 = 14	14 ÷ 7 = 2
6 x 3 = 18	18 ÷ 6 = 3	7 x 3 = 21	21 ÷ 7 = 3
6 x 4 = 24	24 ÷ 6 = 4	7 x 4 = 28	28 ÷ 7 = 4
6 x 5 = 30	30 ÷ 6 = 5	7 x 5 = 35	35 ÷ 7 = 5
6 x 6 = 36	36 ÷ 6 = 6	7 x 6 = 42	42 ÷ 7 = 6
6 x 7 = 42	42 ÷ 6 = 7	7 x 7 = 49	49 ÷ 7 = 7
6 x 8 = 48	48 ÷ 6 = 8	7 x 8 = 56	56 ÷ 7 = 8
6 x 9 = 54	54 ÷ 6 = 9	7 x 9 = 63	63 ÷ 7 = 9

8 x 1 = 8	8 ÷ 8 = 1	9 x 1 = 9	9 ÷ 9 = 1
8 x 2 = 16	16 ÷ 8 = 2	9 x 2 = 18	18 ÷ 9 = 2
8 x 3 = 24	24 ÷ 8 = 3	9 x 3 = 27	27 ÷ 9 = 3
8 x 4 = 32	32 ÷ 8 = 4	9 x 4 = 36	36 ÷ 9 = 4
8 x 5 = 40	40 ÷ 8 = 5	9 x 5 = 45	45 ÷ 9 = 5
8 x 6 = 48	48 ÷ 8 = 6	9 x 6 = 54	54 ÷ 9 = 6
8 x 7 = 56	56 ÷ 8 = 7	9 x 7 = 63	63 ÷ 9 = 7
8 x 8 = 64	64 ÷ 8 = 8	9 x 8 = 72	72 ÷ 9 = 8
8 x 9 = 72	72 ÷ 8 = 9	9 x 9 = 81	81 ÷ 9 = 9

PRACTICE WITH DIVISION FACTS:

2)2	3)9	4)12	5)10	6)6	7)35
8)8	7)14	5)15	4)8	9)9	8)56
2)12	3)6	6)12	7)21	8)24	9)18
3)12	5)25	7)28	9)36	5)45	7)63
3)15	8)48	4)24	9)63	6)42	9)72
2)6	3)27	5)30	7)49	6)18	8)64
6)36	9)45	4)16	2)10	3)21	2)14
4)4	7)7	8)72	3)18	6)48	8)40
2)18	4)36	8)16	9)54	7)42	6)54
5)5	3)3	6)24	8)32	5)40	4)28
9)81	6)30	2)16	3)24	4)32	5)20
2)8	4)20	5)35	9)27	7)56	2)4

PRACTICE WITH DIVISION FACTS:

2)2	3)9	4)12	5)10	6)6	7)35
8)8	7)14	5)15	4)8	9)9	8)56
2)12	3)6	6)12	7)21	8)24	9)18
3)12	5)25	7)28	9)36	5)45	7)63
3)15	8)48	4)24	9)63	6)42	9)72
2)6	3)27	5)30	7)49	6)18	8)64
6)36	9)45	4)16	2)10	3)21	2)14
4)4	7)7	8)72	3)18	6)48	8)40
2)18	4)36	8)16	9)54	7)42	6)54
5)5	3)3	6)24	8)32	5)40	4)28
9)81	6)30	2)16	3)24	4)32	5)20
2)8	4)20	5)35	9)27	7)56	2)4

PRACTICE WITH DIVISION FACTS:

2)2   3)9   4)12   5)10   6)6   7)35

8)8   7)14   5)15   4)8   9)9   8)56

2)12   3)6   6)12   7)21   8)24   9)18

3)12   5)25   7)28   9)36   5)45   7)63

3)15   8)48   4)24   9)63   6)42   9)72

2)6   3)27   5)30   7)49   6)18   8)64

6)36   9)45   4)16   2)10   3)21   2)14

4)4   7)7   8)72   3)18   6)48   8)40

2)18   4)36   8)16   9)54   7)42   6)54

5)5   3)3   6)24   8)32   5)40   4)28

9)81   6)30   2)16   3)24   4)32   5)20

2)8   4)20   5)35   9)27   7)56   2)4

DIVISION — Page 257

$$4\overline{)32} \qquad 2\overline{)18} \qquad 3\overline{)27} \qquad 4\overline{)24} \qquad 5\overline{)35} \qquad 7\overline{)49} \qquad 8\overline{)56}$$

$$6\overline{)48} \qquad 9\overline{)72} \qquad 8\overline{)64} \qquad 9\overline{)63} \qquad 8\overline{)72} \qquad 4\overline{)88} \qquad 3\overline{)69}$$

$$7\overline{)357} \qquad 6\overline{)486} \qquad 9\overline{)549} \qquad 3\overline{)216} \qquad 8\overline{)408} \qquad 2\overline{)148} \qquad 4\overline{)248}$$

$$5\overline{)205} \qquad 7\overline{)427} \qquad 5\overline{)255} \qquad 3\overline{)189} \qquad 9\overline{)729} \qquad 6\overline{)246} \qquad 7\overline{)147}$$

$$4\overline{)168} \qquad 7\overline{)567} \qquad 5\overline{)105} \qquad 3\overline{)156} \qquad 5\overline{)305} \qquad 6\overline{)126} \qquad 7\overline{)147}$$

CHECK YOUR PROBLEMS HERE:
DIVISOR TIMES (X) QUOTIENT = DIVIDEND

DIVISION — Page 257

4)32 2)18 3)27 4)24 5)35 7)49 8)56

6)48 9)72 8)64 9)63 8)72 4)88 3)69

7)357 6)486 9)549 3)216 8)408 2)148 4)248

5)205 7)427 5)255 3)189 9)729 6)246 7)147

4)168 7)567 5)105 3)156 5)305 6)126 7)147

CHECK YOUR PROBLEMS HERE:
DIVISOR TIMES (X) QUOTIENT = DIVIDEND

DIVISION — Page 257

4)32   2)18   3)27   4)24   5)35   7)49   8)56

6)48   9)72   8)64   9)63   8)72   4)88   3)69

7)357   6)486   9)549   3)216   8)408   2)148   4)248

5)205   7)427   5)255   3)189   9)729   6)246   7)147

4)168   7)567   5)105   3)156   5)305   6)126   7)147

CHECK YOUR PROBLEMS HERE:
DIVISOR TIMES (X) QUOTIENT = DIVIDEND

DIVISION —Page 257 Continued.

$9\overline{)189}$ $6\overline{)546}$ $4\overline{)128}$ $8\overline{)248}$ $6\overline{)426}$ $5\overline{)155}$ $4\overline{)364}$

$6\overline{)306}$ $9\overline{)459}$ $3\overline{)126}$ $9\overline{)819}$ $5\overline{)455}$ $6\overline{)186}$ $3\overline{)246}$

$8\overline{)168}$ $7\overline{)217}$ $3\overline{)273}$ $7\overline{)637}$ $2\overline{)104}$ $8\overline{)328}$ $5\overline{)405}$

$2\overline{)122}$ $4\overline{)208}$ $9\overline{)279}$ $7\overline{)497}$ $8\overline{)488}$ $4\overline{)284}$ $2\overline{)184}$

$9\overline{)369}$ $8\overline{)648}$ $7\overline{)287}$ $9\overline{)639}$ $8\overline{)568}$ $4\overline{)328}$ $5\overline{)355}$

Check problems here:

DIVISION —Page 257 Continued.

9)189   6)546   4)128   8)248   6)426   5)155   4)364

6)306   9)459   3)126   9)819   5)455   6)186   3)246

8)168   7)217   3)273   7)637   2)104   8)328   5)405

2)122   4)208   9)279   7)497   8)488   4)284   2)184

9)369   8)648   7)287   9)639   8)568   4)328   5)355

Check problems here:

DIVISION —Page 257 Continued.

9)189   6)546   4)128   8)248   6)426   5)155   4)364

6)306   9)459   3)126   9)819   5)455   6)186   3)246

8)168   7)217   3)273   7)637   2)104   8)328   5)405

2)122   4)208   9)279   7)497   8)488   4)284   2)184

9)369   8)648   7)287   9)639   8)568   4)328   5)355

Check problems here:

TIMED TEST FOR DIVISION FACTS:
[TIME: 2 MIN. 36 SEC.]

$2 \div 2 =$	$3 \div 3 =$	$4 \div 4 =$	$5 \div 5 =$
$4 \div 2 =$	$6 \div 3 =$	$8 \div 4 =$	$10 \div 5 =$
$6 \div 2 =$	$9 \div 3 =$	$12 \div 4 =$	$15 \div 5 =$
$8 \div 2 =$	$12 \div 3 =$	$16 \div 4 =$	$20 \div 5 =$
$10 \div 2 =$	$15 \div 3 =$	$20 \div 4 =$	$25 \div 5 =$
$12 \div 2 =$	$18 \div 3 =$	$24 \div 4 =$	$30 \div 5 =$
$14 \div 2 =$	$21 \div 3 =$	$28 \div 4 =$	$35 \div 5 =$
$16 \div 2 =$	$24 \div 3 =$	$32 \div 4 =$	$40 \div 5 =$
$18 \div 2 =$	$27 \div 3 =$	$36 \div 4 =$	$45 \div 5 =$
$6 \div 6 =$	$7 \div 7 =$	$8 \div 8 =$	$9 \div 9 =$
$12 \div 6 =$	$14 \div 7 =$	$16 \div 8 =$	$18 \div 9 =$
$18 \div 6 =$	$21 \div 7 =$	$24 \div 8 =$	$27 \div 9 =$
$24 \div 6 =$	$28 \div 7 =$	$32 \div 8 =$	$36 \div 9 =$
$30 \div 6 =$	$35 \div 7 =$	$40 \div 8 =$	$45 \div 9 =$
$36 \div 6 =$	$42 \div 7 =$	$48 \div 8 =$	$54 \div 9 =$
$42 \div 6 =$	$49 \div 7 =$	$56 \div 8 =$	$63 \div 9 =$
$48 \div 6 =$	$56 \div 7 =$	$64 \div 8 =$	$72 \div 9 =$
$54 \div 6 =$	$63 \div 7 =$	$72 \div 8 =$	$81 \div 9 =$

Over:
47a
(Blank for practice)

TIMED TEST FOR DIVISION FACTS:
[TIME: 2 MIN. 36 SEC.]

$2 \div 2 =$	$3 \div 3 =$	$4 \div 4 =$	$5 \div 5 =$
$4 \div 2 =$	$6 \div 3 =$	$8 \div 4 =$	$10 \div 5 =$
$6 \div 2 =$	$9 \div 3 =$	$12 \div 4 =$	$15 \div 5 =$
$8 \div 2 =$	$12 \div 3 =$	$16 \div 4 =$	$20 \div 5 =$
$10 \div 2 =$	$15 \div 3 =$	$20 \div 4 =$	$25 \div 5 =$
$12 \div 2 =$	$18 \div 3 =$	$24 \div 4 =$	$30 \div 5 =$
$14 \div 2 =$	$21 \div 3 =$	$28 \div 4 =$	$35 \div 5 =$
$16 \div 2 =$	$24 \div 3 =$	$32 \div 4 =$	$40 \div 5 =$
$18 \div 2 =$	$27 \div 3 =$	$36 \div 4 =$	$45 \div 5 =$
$6 \div 6 =$	$7 \div 7 =$	$8 \div 8 =$	$9 \div 9 =$
$12 \div 6 =$	$14 \div 7 =$	$16 \div 8 =$	$18 \div 9 =$
$18 \div 6 =$	$21 \div 7 =$	$24 \div 8 =$	$27 \div 9 =$
$24 \div 6 =$	$28 \div 7 =$	$32 \div 8 =$	$36 \div 9 =$
$30 \div 6 =$	$35 \div 7 =$	$40 \div 8 =$	$45 \div 9 =$
$36 \div 6 =$	$42 \div 7 =$	$48 \div 8 =$	$54 \div 9 =$
$42 \div 6 =$	$49 \div 7 =$	$56 \div 8 =$	$63 \div 9 =$
$48 \div 6 =$	$56 \div 7 =$	$64 \div 8 =$	$72 \div 9 =$
$54 \div 6 =$	$63 \div 7 =$	$72 \div 8 =$	$81 \div 9 =$

Over:
48a
(Blank for practice)

TIMED TEST FOR DIVISION FACTS:
[TIME: 2 MIN. 36 SEC.]

$2 \div 2 =$	$3 \div 3 =$	$4 \div 4 =$	$5 \div 5 =$
$4 \div 2 =$	$6 \div 3 =$	$8 \div 4 =$	$10 \div 5 =$
$6 \div 2 =$	$9 \div 3 =$	$12 \div 4 =$	$15 \div 5 =$
$8 \div 2 =$	$12 \div 3 =$	$16 \div 4 =$	$20 \div 5 =$
$10 \div 2 =$	$15 \div 3 =$	$20 \div 4 =$	$25 \div 5 =$
$12 \div 2 =$	$18 \div 3 =$	$24 \div 4 =$	$30 \div 5 =$
$14 \div 2 =$	$21 \div 3 =$	$28 \div 4 =$	$35 \div 5 =$
$16 \div 2 =$	$24 \div 3 =$	$32 \div 4 =$	$40 \div 5 =$
$18 \div 2 =$	$27 \div 3 =$	$36 \div 4 =$	$45 \div 5 =$
$6 \div 6 =$	$7 \div 7 =$	$8 \div 8 =$	$9 \div 9 =$
$12 \div 6 =$	$14 \div 7 =$	$16 \div 8 =$	$18 \div 9 =$
$18 \div 6 =$	$21 \div 7 =$	$24 \div 8 =$	$27 \div 9 =$
$24 \div 6 =$	$28 \div 7 =$	$32 \div 8 =$	$36 \div 9 =$
$30 \div 6 =$	$35 \div 7 =$	$40 \div 8 =$	$45 \div 9 =$
$36 \div 6 =$	$42 \div 7 =$	$48 \div 8 =$	$54 \div 9 =$
$42 \div 6 =$	$49 \div 7 =$	$56 \div 8 =$	$63 \div 9 =$
$48 \div 6 =$	$56 \div 7 =$	$64 \div 8 =$	$72 \div 9 =$
$54 \div 6 =$	$63 \div 7 =$	$72 \div 8 =$	$81 \div 9 =$

Over:
49a
(Blank for practice)

TIMED TEST FOR DIVISION FACTS:
[TIME: 2 MIN. 36 SEC.]

2)2	3)9	4)12	5)10	6)6	7)35
8)8	7)14	5)15	4)8	9)9	8)56
2)12	3)6	6)12	7)21	8)24	9)18
3)12	5)25	7)28	9)36	5)45	7)63
3)15	8)48	4)24	9)63	6)42	9)72
2)6	3)27	5)30	7)49	6)18	8)64
6)36	9)45	4)16	2)10	3)21	2)14
4)4	7)7	8)72	3)18	6)48	8)40
2)18	4)36	8)16	9)54	7)42	6)54
5)5	3)3	6)24	8)32	5)40	4)28
9)81	6)30	2)16	3)24	4)32	5)20
2)8	4)20	5)35	9)27	7)56	2)4

TIMED TEST FOR DIVISION FACTS:
[TIME: 2 MIN. 36 SEC.]

2)2	3)9	4)12	5)10	6)6	7)35
8)8	7)14	5)15	4)8	9)9	8)56
2)12	3)6	6)12	7)21	8)24	9)18
3)12	5)25	7)28	9)36	5)45	7)63
3)15	8)48	4)24	9)63	6)42	9)72
2)6	3)27	5)30	7)49	6)18	8)64
6)36	9)45	4)16	2)10	3)21	2)14
4)4	7)7	8)72	3)18	6)48	8)40
2)18	4)36	8)16	9)54	7)42	6)54
5)5	3)3	6)24	8)32	5)40	4)28
9)81	6)30	2)16	3)24	4)32	5)20
2)8	4)20	5)35	9)27	7)56	2)4

Over:
51a
(Blank for practice)

TIMED TEST FOR DIVISION FACTS:
[TIME: 2 MIN. 36 SEC.]

2)2   3)9   4)12   5)10   6)6   7)35

8)8   7)14   5)15   4)8   9)9   8)56

2)12   3)6   6)12   7)21   8)24   9)18

3)12   5)25   7)28   9)36   5)45   7)63

3)15   8)48   4)24   9)63   6)42   9)72

2)6   3)27   5)30   7)49   6)18   8)64

6)36   9)45   4)16   2)10   3)21   2)14

4)4   7)7   8)72   3)18   6)48   8)40

2)18   4)36   8)16   9)54   7)42   6)54

5)5   3)3   6)24   8)32   5)40   4)28

9)81   6)30   2)16   3)24   4)32   5)20

2)8   4)20   5)35   9)27   7)56   2)4

Over:
52a
(Blank for practice)

Division with remainder Page 259.

$2\overline{)5}$ $2\overline{)7}$ $2\overline{)9}$ $2\overline{)11}$ $2\overline{)15}$ $2\overline{)17}$ $2\overline{)19}$

$3\overline{)7}$ $3\overline{)10}$ $3\overline{)13}$ $3\overline{)19}$ $3\overline{)22}$ $3\overline{)25}$ $3\overline{)29}$

$4\overline{)6}$ $4\overline{)9}$ $4\overline{)15}$ $4\overline{)21}$ $4\overline{)27}$ $4\overline{)30}$ $4\overline{)39}$

$5\overline{)13}$ $5\overline{)22}$ $5\overline{)31}$ $5\overline{)37}$ $5\overline{)39}$ $5\overline{)43}$ $5\overline{)48}$

$6\overline{)15}$ $6\overline{)19}$ $6\overline{)21}$ $6\overline{)28}$ $6\overline{)33}$ $6\overline{)37}$ $6\overline{)40}$

$6\overline{)45}$ $6\overline{)50}$ $6\overline{)55}$ $6\overline{)57}$ $6\overline{)59}$

Division with remainder Page 259.

$2\overline{)5}$ $2\overline{)7}$ $2\overline{)9}$ $2\overline{)11}$ $2\overline{)15}$ $2\overline{)17}$ $2\overline{)19}$

$3\overline{)7}$ $3\overline{)10}$ $3\overline{)13}$ $3\overline{)19}$ $3\overline{)22}$ $3\overline{)25}$ $3\overline{)29}$

$4\overline{)6}$ $4\overline{)9}$ $4\overline{)15}$ $4\overline{)21}$ $4\overline{)27}$ $4\overline{)30}$ $4\overline{)39}$

$5\overline{)13}$ $5\overline{)22}$ $5\overline{)31}$ $5\overline{)37}$ $5\overline{)39}$ $5\overline{)43}$ $5\overline{)48}$

$6\overline{)15}$ $6\overline{)19}$ $6\overline{)21}$ $6\overline{)28}$ $6\overline{)33}$ $6\overline{)37}$ $6\overline{)40}$

$6\overline{)45}$ $6\overline{)50}$ $6\overline{)55}$ $6\overline{)57}$ $6\overline{)59}$

Division with remainder Page 259.

2)5   2)7   2)9   2)11   2)15   2)17   2)19

3)7   3)10   3)13   3)19   3)22   3)25   3)29

4)6   4)9   4)15   4)21   4)27   4)30   4)39

5)13   5)22   5)31   5)37   5)39   5)43   5)48

6)15   6)19   6)21   6)28   6)33   6)37   6)40

6)45   6)50   6)55   6)57   6)59

Division with remainder Page 259 Continued.

$7)\overline{13}$ $7)\overline{16}$ $7)\overline{20}$ $7)\overline{25}$ $7)\overline{30}$ $7)\overline{34}$ $7)\overline{40}$

$7)\overline{47}$ $7)\overline{51}$ $7)\overline{55}$ $7)\overline{58}$ $7)\overline{62}$ $7)\overline{65}$ $7)\overline{68}$

$8)\overline{18}$ $8)\overline{28}$ $8)\overline{31}$ $8)\overline{44}$ $8)\overline{47}$ $8)\overline{51}$ $8)\overline{55}$

$8)\overline{58}$ $8)\overline{60}$ $8)\overline{65}$ $8)\overline{68}$ $8)\overline{70}$ $8)\overline{73}$ $8)\overline{77}$

$9)\overline{12}$ $9)\overline{17}$ $9)\overline{21}$ $9)\overline{26}$ $9)\overline{32}$ $9)\overline{35}$ $9)\overline{40}$

$9)\overline{44}$ $9)\overline{48}$ $9)\overline{52}$ $9)\overline{55}$ $9)\overline{60}$ $9)\overline{62}$ $9)\overline{65}$

$9)\overline{69}$ $9)\overline{71}$ $9)\overline{75}$ $9)\overline{79}$ $9)\overline{83}$ $9)\overline{85}$ $9)\overline{87}$

Division with remainder Page 259 Continued.

$7\overline{)13}$ $7\overline{)16}$ $7\overline{)20}$ $7\overline{)25}$ $7\overline{)30}$ $7\overline{)34}$ $7\overline{)40}$

$7\overline{)47}$ $7\overline{)51}$ $7\overline{)55}$ $7\overline{)58}$ $7\overline{)62}$ $7\overline{)65}$ $7\overline{)68}$

$8\overline{)18}$ $8\overline{)28}$ $8\overline{)31}$ $8\overline{)44}$ $8\overline{)47}$ $8\overline{)51}$ $8\overline{)55}$

$8\overline{)58}$ $8\overline{)60}$ $8\overline{)65}$ $8\overline{)68}$ $8\overline{)70}$ $8\overline{)73}$ $8\overline{)77}$

$9\overline{)12}$ $9\overline{)17}$ $9\overline{)21}$ $9\overline{)26}$ $9\overline{)32}$ $9\overline{)35}$ $9\overline{)40}$

$9\overline{)44}$ $9\overline{)48}$ $9\overline{)52}$ $9\overline{)55}$ $9\overline{)60}$ $9\overline{)62}$ $9\overline{)65}$

$9\overline{)69}$ $9\overline{)71}$ $9\overline{)75}$ $9\overline{)79}$ $9\overline{)83}$ $9\overline{)85}$ $9\overline{)87}$

Division with remainder Page 259 Continued.

7)13   7)16   7)20   7)25   7)30   7)34   7)40

7)47   7)51   7)55   7)58   7)62   7)65   7)68

8)18   8)28   8)31   8)44   8)47   8)51   8)55

8)58   8)60   8)65   8)68   8)70   8)73   8)77

9)12   9)17   9)21   9)26   9)32   9)35   9)40

9)44   9)48   9)52   9)55   9)60   9)62   9)65

9)69   9)71   9)75   9)79   9)83   9)85   9)87

Division with carrying without remainders. Page 261

How many 3's
go into 8? Two.

```
     2
  3)84
  6
```

Bring down 4

```
     2
  3)84
  6˅
  24
```

Check:

```
  28
  x3
  84
```

How many 3's
go into 24?
Eight.

```
    28
  3)84
  6˅
  24
  24
```

2)56   2)74   2)138   2)156   2)178   2)194

3)78   3)81   3)195   3)234   3)258   3)297

4)76   4)96   4)268   4)296   4)356   4)392

5)95   5)135   5)190   5)245   5)315   5)420

CHECK:

Division with carrying without remainders. Page 261

How many 3's go into 8? Two.

```
  2
3)84
  6
```

Bring down 4

```
  2
3)84
  6˘
  24
```

Check:
```
 28
 x3
 84
```

How many 3's go into 24? Eight.

```
 28
3)84
 6˘
 24
 24
```

2)56   2)74   2)138   2)156   2)178   2)194

3)78   3)81   3)195   3)234   3)258   3)297

4)76   4)96   4)268   4)296   4)356   4)392

5)95   5)135   5)190   5)245   5)315   5)420

CHECK:

Division with carrying without remainders. Page 261

How many 3's
go into 8? Two.

$$3\overline{)84}$$
2
6

Bring down 4

$$3\overline{)84}$$
2
6˘
24

Check: 28
x3
84

How many 3's
go into 24?
Eight.

$$3\overline{)84}$$
28
6˘
24
24

2)56   2)74   2)138   2)156   2)178   2)194

3)78   3)81   3)195   3)234   3)258   3)297

4)76   4)96   4)268   4)296   4)356   4)392

5)95   5)135   5)190   5)245   5)315   5)420

CHECK:

Division with carrying without remainders. Page 261 Continued.

How many 3's go into 8? Two.

$$3)\overline{84}$$ with 2 above, 6

Bring down 4

$$3)\overline{84}$$ 2 above, 6, 24

Check: 28 ×3 84

How many 3's go into 24? Eight.

$$3)\overline{84}$$ 28 above, 6, 24, 24

$6)\overline{156}$ $6)\overline{198}$ $6)\overline{264}$ $6)\overline{396}$ $6)\overline{444}$ $6)\overline{594}$

$7)\overline{196}$ $7)\overline{252}$ $7)\overline{315}$ $7)\overline{406}$ $7)\overline{553}$ $7)\overline{679}$

$8)\overline{256}$ $8)\overline{352}$ $8)\overline{472}$ $8)\overline{544}$ $8)\overline{696}$ $8)\overline{784}$

$9)\overline{351}$ $9)\overline{477}$ $9)\overline{585}$ $9)\overline{702}$ $9)\overline{774}$ $9)\overline{891}$

Division with carrying without remainders. Page 261 Continued.

How many 3's
go into 8? Two.

```
      2
    3)84
      6
```

Bring down 4

```
      2
    3)84
      6˘
      24
```

Check:
```
    28
    x3
    84
```

How many 3's
go into 24?
Eight.

```
      28
    3)84
      6˘
      24
      24
```

6)156   6)198   6)264   6)396   6)444   6)594

7)196   7)252   7)315   7)406   7)553   7)679

8)256   8)352   8)472   8)544   8)696   8)784

9)351   9)477   9)585   9)702   9)774   9)891

Division with carrying without remainders. Page 261
Continued.

How many 3's
go into 8? Two.

```
  2
3)84
  6
```

Bring down 4

```
  2
3)84
  6ˇ
 24
```

Check:

```
 28
 x3
 84
```

How many 3's
go into 24?
Eight.

```
 28
3)84
  6ˇ
 24
 24
```

6)156   6)198   6)264   6)396   6)444   6)594

7)196   7)252   7)315   7)406   7)553   7)679

8)256   8)352   8)472   8)544   8)696   8)784

9)351   9)477   9)585   9)702   9)774   9)891

DIVISION WITH REMAINDERS. PAGE 261 AND 262.

How many 3's go
into 8? Two.

```
  2
3)89
  6
  2
```

Bring down 9.

```
  2
3)89
  6ˇ
  29
```

How many 3's go
into 29? Nine with
a remainder of 2.

```
 29
3)89
 6ˇ
 29
 27
  2
```

Check:

```
 29
 x3
 87
 ±2
 89
```

3)206   7)325   5)172   2)31   6)224   4)311

8)217   4)139   9)716   3)74   6)334   7)132

9)318   5)284   6)115   2)75   3)239   8)412

7)197   3)172   9)832   4)50   5)391   6)279

DIVISION WITH REMAINDERS. PAGE 261 AND 262.

How many 3's go into 8? Two.

```
  2
3)89
  6
  2
```

Bring down 9.

```
  2
3)89
  6ˇ
  29
```

How many 3's go into 29? Nine with a remainder of 2.

```
  29
3)89
  6ˇ
  29
  27
   2
```

Check:

```
  29
  x3
  87
  ±2
  89
```

3)206   7)325   5)172   2)31   6)224   4)311

8)217   4)139   9)716   3)74   6)334   7)132

9)318   5)284   6)115   2)75   3)239   8)412

7)197   3)172   9)832   4)50   5)391   6)279

DIVISION WITH REMAINDERS. PAGE 261 AND 262.

How many 3's go
into 8? Two.

```
  2
3)89
  6
  2
```

Bring down 9.

```
  2
3)89
  6ˇ
 29
```

How many 3's go
into 29? Nine with
a remainder of 2.

```
 29
3)89
  6ˇ
 29
 27
  2
```

Check:

```
 29
 x3
 87
 ±2
 89
```

3)206   7)325   5)172   2)31   6)224   4)311

8)217   4)139   9)716   3)74   6)334   7)132

9)318   5)284   6)115   2)75   3)239   8)412

7)197   3)172   9)832   4)50   5)391   6)279

DIVISION WITH REMAINDERS. PAGE 261 AND 262.
Continued.

How many 3's go
into 8? Two.

```
  2
3)89
  6
  2
```

Bring down 9.

```
  2
3)89
  6˘
  29
```

How many 3's go
into 29? Nine with
a remainder of 2.

```
 29
3)89
 6˘
 29
 27
  2
```

Check:

```
 29
 x3
 87
 ±2
 89
```

4)387   5)473   8)306   2)97   7)389   3)40

7)261   9)415   8)395   5)63   6)169   8)129

2)119   4)225   9)732   2)53   8)765   5)116

Don't forget to check your answers.

DIVISION WITH REMAINDERS. PAGE 261 AND 262. Continued.

How many 3's go into 8? Two.

```
  2
3)89
  6
  2
```

Bring down 9.

```
  2
3)89
  6ˇ
  29
```

How many 3's go into 29? Nine with a remainder of 2.

```
 29
3)89
  6ˇ
  29
  27
   2
```

Check:

```
 29
 x3
 87
 ±2
 89
```

```
4)387    5)473    8)306    2)97    7)389    3)40
```

```
7)261    9)415    8)395    5)63    6)169    8)129
```

```
2)119    4)225    9)732    2)53    8)765    5)116
```

Don't forget to check your answers.

DIVISION WITH REMAINDERS. PAGE 261 AND 262.
Continued.

How many 3's go
into 8? Two.

```
  2
3)89
  6
  2
```

Bring down 9.

```
  2
3)89
  6
 29
```

How many 3's go
into 29? Nine with
a remainder of 2.

```
 29
3)89
  6
 29
 27
  2
```

Check:

```
 29
 x3
 87
 ±2
 89
```

4)387   5)473   8)306   2)97   7)389   3)40

7)261   9)415   8)395   5)63   6)169   8)129

2)119   4)225   9)732   2)53   8)765   5)116

Don't forget to check your answers.

DIVISION WITH 3-DIGIT QUOTIENTS. PAGE 262

Example:

```
        186
     5)933
        5ˇ
        43
        40ˇ
        33
        30
     3 Remainder
```

Check:
```
  186
  x 5
  930
  + 3
  933
```

5)933   3)2810   2)972   6)5591   8)3087   4)1077

9)2550   2)719   7)4490   3)741   9)6831   6)1724

8)1395   6)2740   4)734   4)2299

DIVISION WITH 3-DIGIT QUOTIENTS. PAGE 262

Example:
```
        186
     5)933
       5ˇ
       43
       40ˇ
        33
        30
       3 Remainder
```

Check:
```
     186
      x 5
     930
     + 3
     933
```

5)933   3)2810   2)972   6)5591   8)3087   4)1077

9)2550   2)719   7)4490   3)741   9)6831   6)1724

8)1395   6)2740   4)734   4)2299

DIVISION WITH 3-DIGIT QUOTIENTS. PAGE 262

Example:

```
        186
     5)933
       5ˇ
       43
       40ˇ
       33
       30
      3 Remainder
```

Check:
```
  186
  x 5
  930
  + 3
  933
```

5)933   3)2810   2)972   6)5591   8)3087   4)1077

9)2550   2)719   7)4490   3)741   9)6831   6)1724

8)1395   6)2740   4)734   4)2299

DIVISION WITH 3-DIGIT QUOTIENTS. PAGE 262 Cont'd.

Example:
```
         186
      5)933
        5˅
        43
        40˅
        33
        30
        3 Remainder
```

Check:
```
   186
   x 5
   930
   + 3
   933
```

```
5)2862    7)6705    9)5776    2)592    5)1974    4)931
```

```
8)2156    7)4545    9)7097    6)5921    2)40    2)204
```

```
2)2004    2)41    3)62    2)410    3)621    3)322
```

DIVISION WITH 3-DIGIT QUOTIENTS. PAGE 262 Cont'd.

Example:

```
        186
     5)933
        5ˇ
        43
        40ˇ
        33
        30
     3 Remainder
```

Check:
```
      186
      x 5
      930
      + 3
      933
```

5)2862   7)6705   9)5776   2)592   5)1974   4)931

8)2156   7)4545   9)7097   6)5921   2)40   2)204

2)2004   2)41   3)62   2)410   3)621   3)322

DIVISION WITH 3-DIGIT QUOTIENTS. PAGE 262 Cont'd.

Example:
```
      186
   5)933
      5ˇ
      43
      40ˇ
      33
      30
      3 Remainder
```

Check:
```
   186
    x 5
   930
   + 3
   933
```

5)2862   7)6705   9)5776   2)592   5)1974   4)931

8)2156   7)4545   9)7097   6)5921   2)40   2)204

2)2004   2)41   3)62   2)410   3)621   3)322

DIVISION WITH 3-DIGIT QUOTIENTS. PAGE 263 Cont'd.

3)622   4)819   4)962   5)654   6)605   7)4214

8)7265   9)8156   7)3563   6)4838   5)1043   8)5610

9)5436   3)3232   4)3625   6)4082   7)286   8)3841

5)901   9)187   7)3546   9)6316

DIVISION WITH 3-DIGIT QUOTIENTS. PAGE 263 Cont'd.

3)622   4)819   4)962   5)654   6)605   7)4214

8)7265   9)8156   7)3563   6)4838   5)1043   8)5610

9)5436   3)3232   4)3625   6)4082   7)286   8)3841

5)901   9)187   7)3546   9)6316

DIVISION WITH 3-DIGIT QUOTIENTS. PAGE 263 Cont'd.

$3\overline{)622}$ $4\overline{)819}$ $4\overline{)962}$ $5\overline{)654}$ $6\overline{)605}$ $7\overline{)4214}$

$8\overline{)7265}$ $9\overline{)8156}$ $7\overline{)3563}$ $6\overline{)4838}$ $5\overline{)1043}$ $8\overline{)5610}$

$9\overline{)5436}$ $3\overline{)3232}$ $4\overline{)3625}$ $6\overline{)4082}$ $7\overline{)286}$ $8\overline{)3841}$

$5\overline{)901}$ $9\overline{)187}$ $7\overline{)3546}$ $9\overline{)6316}$

ANSWERS

ANSWERS FOR DIVISION PROBLEMS

Answers for problems page labeled 257:

Row 1: 8, 9, 9, 6, 7, 7, 7
Row 2: 8, 9, 8, 7, 9, 22, 23
Row 3: 51, 81, 61, 72, 51, 74, 62
Row 4: 51, 61, 51, 63, 91, 41, 21
Row 5: 42, 81, 21, 52, 61, 21, 21

Answers for problems on page labeled 257 Continued:

Row 1: 21, 91, 32, 31, 71, 31, 91
Row 2: 51, 51, 42, 91, 91, 31, 82
Row 3: 21, 31, 91, 91, 52, 41, 81
Row 4: 61, 52, 31, 71, 61, 71, 92
Row 5: 41, 81, 41, 71, 71, 82, 71

Answers for problems on page labeled 259:

Row 1: 2 R1, 3 R1, 4 R1, 5 R1, 7 R1, 8 R1, 9 R1
Row 2: 2 R1, 3 R1, 4 R1, 6 R1, 7 R1, 8 R1, 9 R2
Row 3: 1 R2, 2 R1, 3 R3, 5 R1, 6 R3, 7 R2, 9 R3
Row 4: 2 R3, 4 R2, 6 R1, 7 R2, 7 R4, 8 R3, 9 R3
Row 5: 2 R3, 3 R1, 3 R3, 4 R4, 5 R3, 6 R1, 6 R4
Row 6: 7 R3, 8 R2, 9 R1, 9 R3, 9 R5

Answers for problems on page labeled 259 Continued:

Row 1: 1 R6, 2 R2, 2 R6, 3 R4, 4 R2, 4 R6, 5 R5
Row 2: 6 R5, 7 R2, 7 R6, 8 R2, 8 R6, 9 R2, 9 R5
Row 3: 2 R2, 3 R4, 3 R7, 5 R4, 5 R7, 6 R3, 6 R7
Row 4: 7 R2, 7 R4, 8 R1, 8 R4, 8 R6, 9 R1, 9 R5
Row 5: 1 R3, 1 R8, 2 R3, 2 R8, 3 R5, 3 R8, 4 R4
Row 6: 4 R8, 5 R3, 5 R7, 6 R1, 6 R6, 6 R8, 7 R2
Row 7: 7 R6, 7 R8, 8 R3, 8 R7, 9 R2, 9 R4, 9 R6

Answers for problems on page labeled 261:

Row 1: 28, 37, 69, 78, 89, 97
Row 2: 26, 27, 65, 78, 86, 99
Row 3: 19, 24, 67, 74, 89, 98
Row 4: 19, 27, 38, 49, 63, 84

Answers for problems on page labeled 261 Continued:
Row 1: 26, 33, 44, 66, 74, 99   Row 3: 32, 44, 59, 68, 87,98
Row 2: 28, 36, 45, 58, 79, 97   Row 4: 39, 53, 65, 78, 86, 99

ANSWERS FOR DIVISION PROBLEMS

Answers for problems on page labeled 261 and 262:
Row 1: 68 R2, 46 R3, 34 R2, 15 R1, 37 R2, 77 R3
Row 2: 27 R1, 34 R3, 79 R5, 24 R2, 55 R4, 18 R6
Row 3: 35 R3, 56 R4, 19 R1, 37 R1, 79 R2, 51 R4
Row 4: 28 R1, 57 R1, 92 R4, 12 R2, 78 R1, 46 R3

Answers for problems on page labeled 261 and 262 Continued:

Row 1: 96 R3, 94 R3, 38 R2, 48 R1, 55 R4, 13 R1
Row 2: 37 R2, 46 R1, 49 R3, 12 R3, 28 R1, 16 R1
Row 3: 59 R1, 56 R1, 81 R3, 26 R1, 95 R5, 23 R1

Answers for problems on page labeled 3 Dig. Quo. Page 262:

Row 1: 186 R3, 936 R2, 486, 931 R5, 385 R7, 269 R1
Row 2: 283 R3, 359 R1, 641 R3, 247, 759, 287 R2
Row 3: 174 R3, 456 R4, 183 R2, 574 R3, 185 R1, 283 R5

Answers for problems on page labeled 3 Dig. Quo. 262 Continued

Row 1: 572 R2, 957 R6, 641 R7, 296, 394 R4, 232 R3
Row 2: 269 R4, 649 R2, 788 R5, 986 R5, 20, 102
Row 3: 1002, 20 R1, 20 R2, 205, 207, 107 R1

Answers for problems on page labeled 263 Continued:

Row 1: 207 R1, 204 R3, 240 R2, 130 R4, 100 R5, 602
Row 2: 908 R1, 906 R2, 509, 806 R2, 208 R3, 701 R2
Row 3: 604, 1077 R1, 906 R1, 680 R2, 40 R6. 480 R1
Row 4: 180 R1, 20 R7, 506 R4, 701 R7

FRACTIONS / FRACTIONS

Fractions — Practice in recognizing fractions

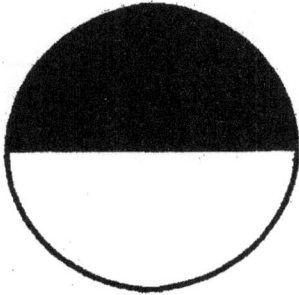

$\frac{1}{2}$ $\frac{1}{3}$

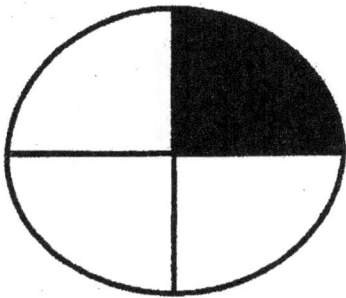

$\frac{1}{4}$ $\frac{1}{8}$

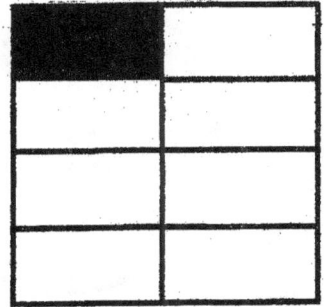

$\frac{1}{5}$ $\frac{1}{10}$

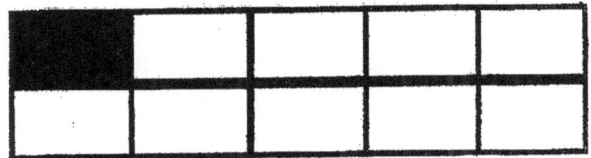

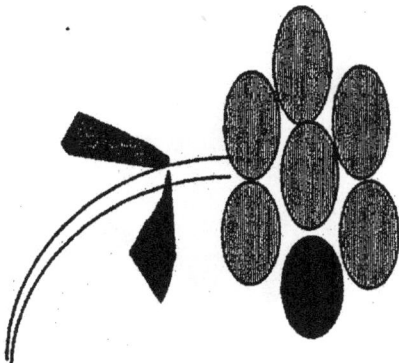

$\frac{1}{7}$

Fractions — Practice in recognizing fractions
Color in fractions

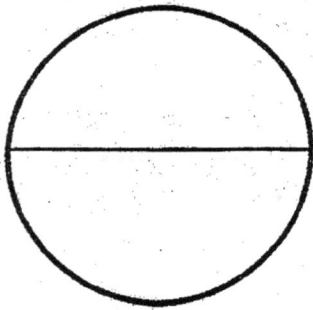

$\frac{1}{2}$ $\frac{1}{3}$

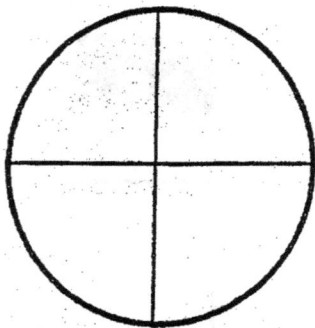

$\frac{1}{4}$ $\frac{1}{8}$

 $\frac{1}{5}$ $\frac{1}{10}$

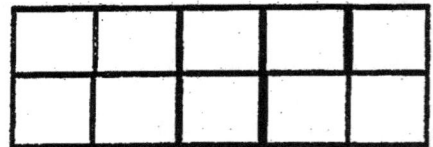

 $\frac{1}{7}$

Fractions — Practice in recognizing fractions
Color in fractions

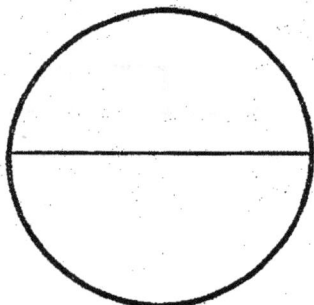
$\dfrac{1}{2}$
$\dfrac{1}{3}$

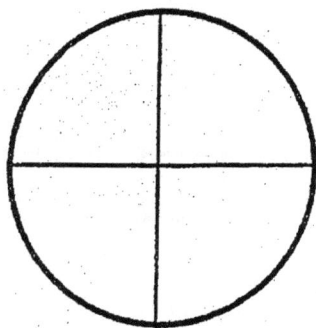
$\dfrac{1}{4}$
$\dfrac{1}{8}$

$\dfrac{1}{5}$
$\dfrac{1}{10}$

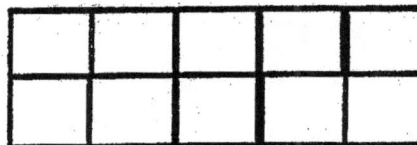

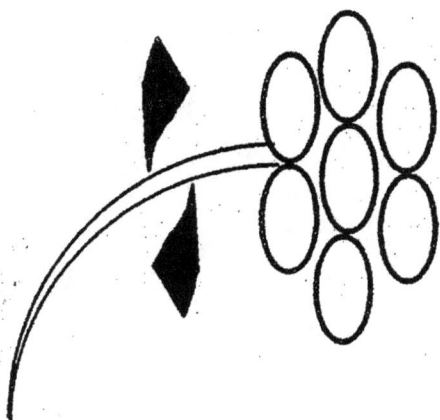
$\dfrac{1}{7}$

Fractions — Practice in recognizing fractions
Color in fractions

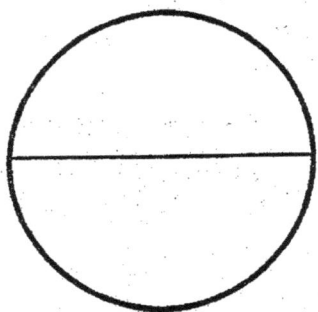

$\dfrac{1}{2}$ $\dfrac{1}{3}$

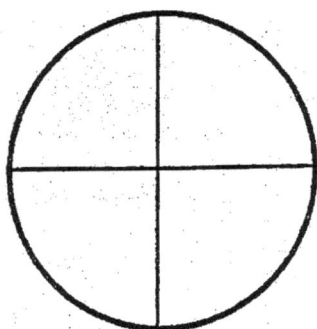

$\dfrac{1}{4}$ $\dfrac{1}{8}$

 $\dfrac{1}{5}$ $\dfrac{1}{10}$

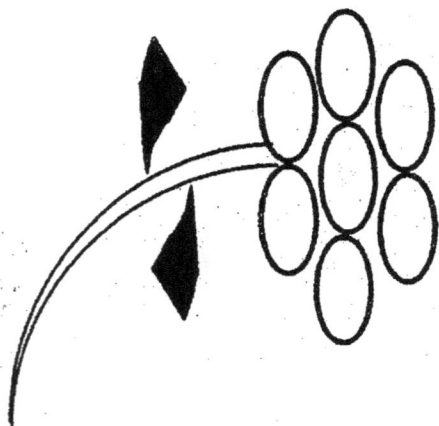 $\dfrac{1}{7}$

FRACTIONS — Practice in recognizing fractions.

COLOR IN $\frac{2}{6}$

$\frac{1}{6}$

COLOR IN $\frac{3}{9}$

$\frac{1}{9}$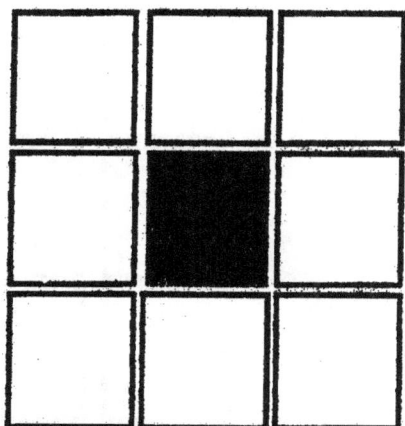

COLOR IN $\frac{2}{3}$

$\frac{2}{3}$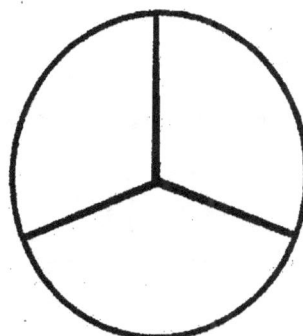

FRACTIONS — Practice in recognizing fractions.

COLOR IN $\frac{2}{6}$

$\frac{1}{6}$

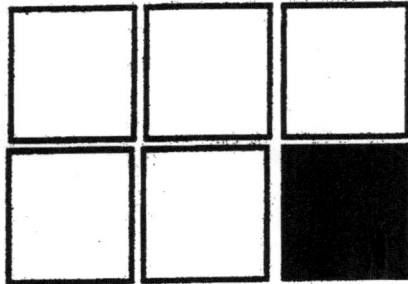

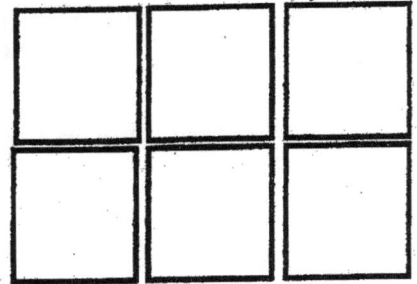

COLOR IN $\frac{3}{9}$

$\frac{1}{9}$

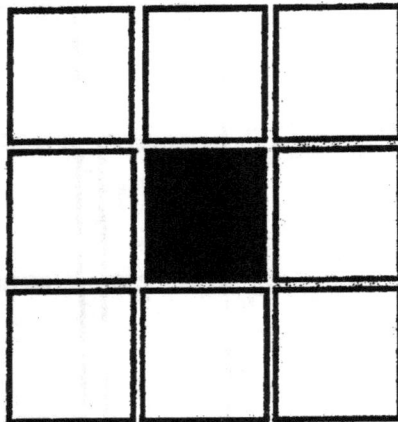

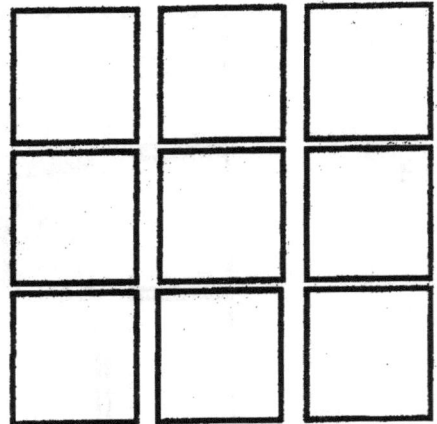

COLOR IN $\frac{2}{3}$

$\frac{2}{3}$

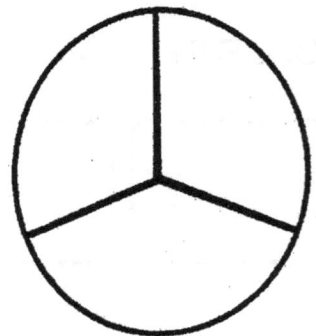

FRACTIONS — Practice in recognizing fractions.

COLOR IN $\frac{2}{6}$

$\frac{1}{6}$

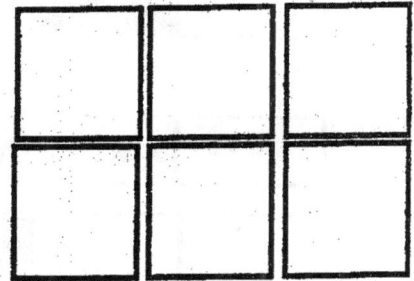

COLOR IN $\frac{3}{9}$

$\frac{1}{9}$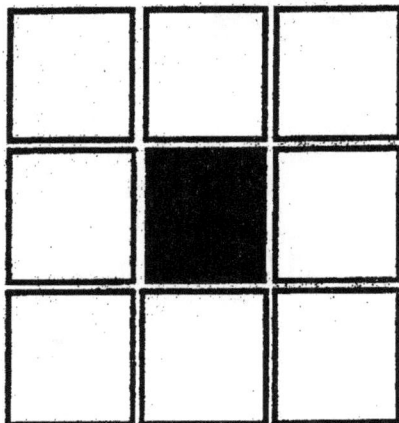

COLOR IN $\frac{2}{3}$

$\frac{2}{3}$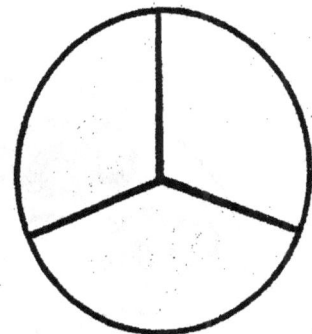

FRACTIONS — PRACTICE RECOGNIZING EQUAL FRACTIONS

 1/2 =

 2/4 =

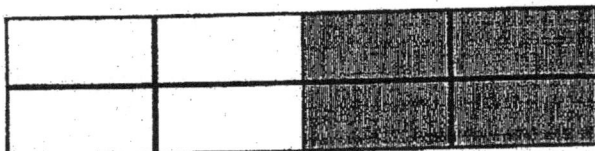 4/8 =

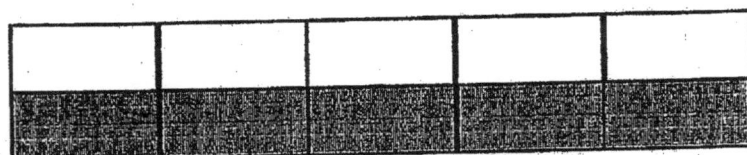 5/10

 1/3 =

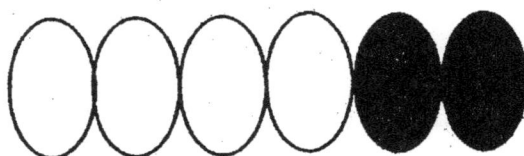 2/6 =

4/12

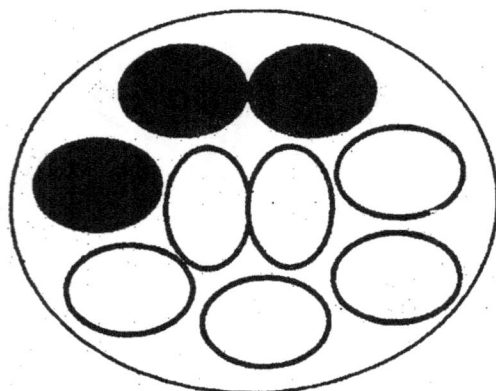 3/9 =

FRACTIONS — PRACTICE RECOGNIZING EQUAL FRACTIONS
COLOR IN

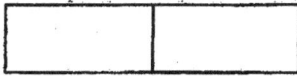 1/2 =

 2/4 =

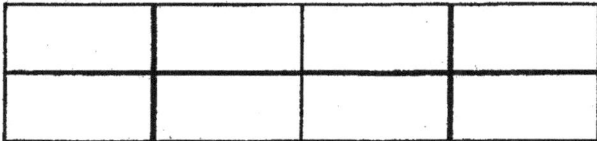 4/8 =

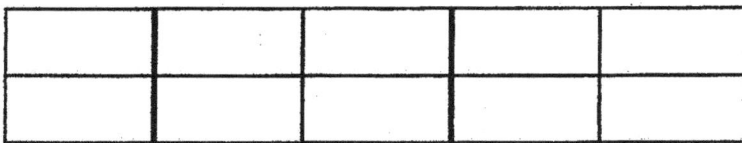 5/10

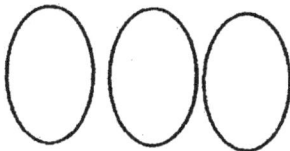 1/3 =

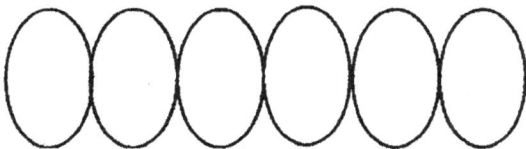 2/6 =

4/12

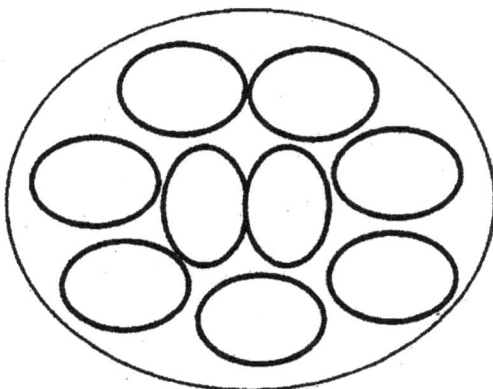 3/9 =

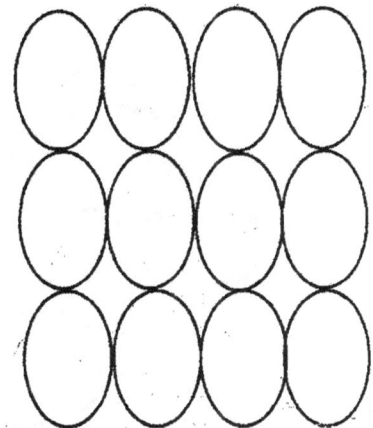

FRACTIONS — PRACTICE RECOGNIZING EQUAL
COLOR IN
FRACTIONS

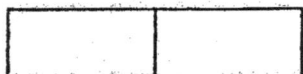 1/2 =

 2/4 =

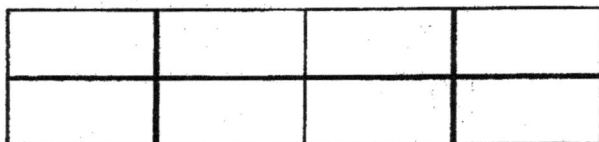 4/8 =

 5/10

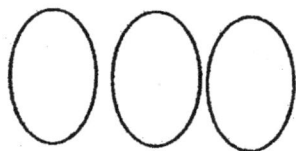 1/3 =

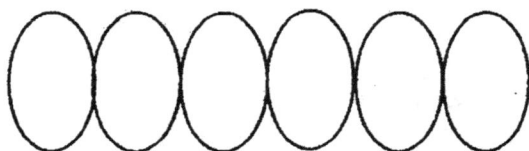 2/6 =

4/12

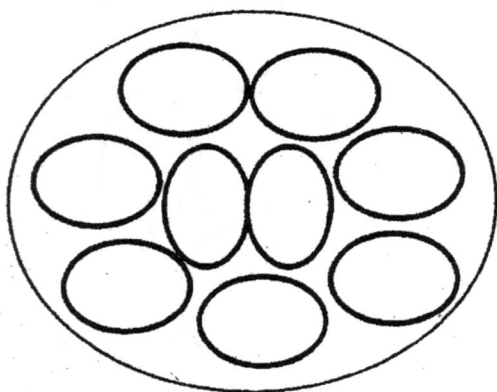 3/9 =

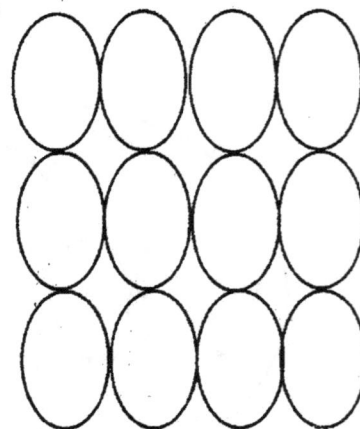

FRACTIONS — PRACTICE RECOGNIZING EQUAL FRACTIONS
COLOR IN

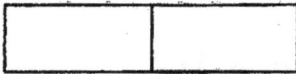 1/2 =

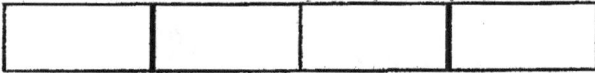 2/4 =

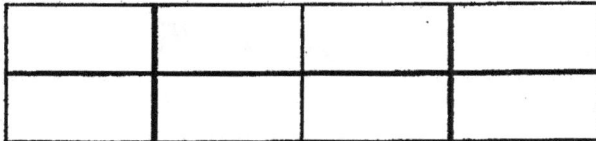 4/8 =

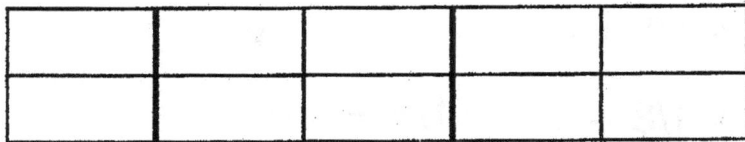 5/10

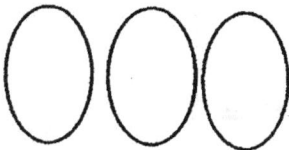 1/3 =

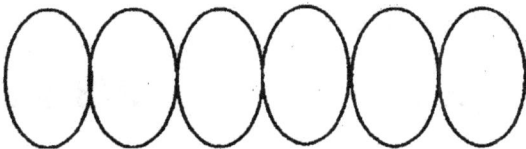 2/6 =

4/12

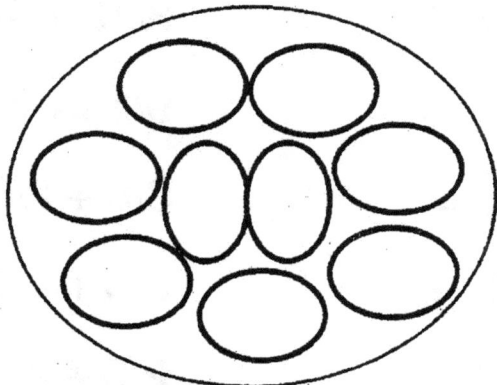 3/9 =

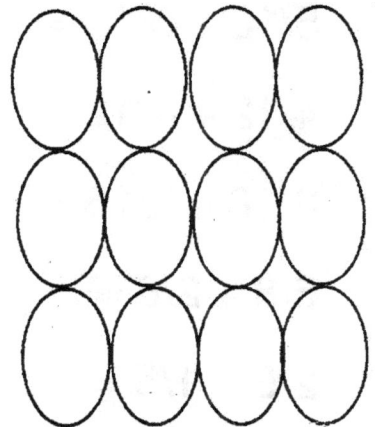

FRACTIONS — ADDING UNIT FRACTIONS, PAGE 265
1 = NUMERATOR   2 = DENOMINATOR   WRITE: 1/2

Add numerators only

$1/3 + 1/3 = 2/3$ $1/4 + 1/4 = 2/4 = 1/2$

$1/4 + 1/4 + 1/4 = 3/4$ $1/8 + 1/8 + 1/8 = 3/8$

$1/5 + 1/5 = 2/5$ $1/5 + 1/5 + 1/5 = 3/5$

$1/5 + 1/5 + 1/5 + 1/5 = 4/5$

$1/8 + 1/8 + 1/8 + 1/8 + 1/8 = 5/8$

$1/8 + 1/8 + 1/8 + 1/8 + 1/8 + 1/8 + 1/8 = 7/8$

$2/5 + 1/5 = 3/5$ $3/5 + 1/5 = 4/5$

$2/5 + 2/5 = 4/5$ $4/5 + 1/5 = 5/5 = 1$

$3/8 + 3/8 + 1/8 = 7/8$ $7/8 + 1/8 = 8/8 = 1$

Fill in the answers for problems below:

$1/3 + 1/3 =$ $2/4 + 1/4 =$ $3/8 + 3/8 =$

$5/16 + 6/16 =$ $2/5 + 2/5 =$ $7/8 + 1/8 =$

$4/12 + 4/12 =$ $6/12 + 5/12 =$ $3/12 + 4/12 =$

$8/16 + 2/16 =$ $3/16 + 5/16 =$ $9/16 + 5/16 =$

$5/8 + 2/8 =$ $4/8 + 2/8 =$ $3/8 + 2/8 =$

$2/5 + 1/5 =$ $4/5 + 1/5 =$ $3/5 + 1/5 =$

$3/6 + 2/6 =$ $4/6 + 1/6 =$ $2/6 + 2/6 =$

FRACTIONS — ADDING UNIT FRACTIONS, PAGE 265
1 = NUMERATOR   2 = DENOMINATOR   WRITE: 1/2

Add numerators only

$1/3 + 1/3 = 2/3$ $1/4 + 1/4 = 2/4 = 1/2$

$1/4 + 1/4 + 1/4 = 3/4$ $1/8 + 1/8 + 1/8 = 3/8$

$1/5 + 1/5 = 2/5$ $1/5 + 1/5 + 1/5 = 3/5$

$1/5 + 1/5 + 1/5 + 1/5 = 4/5$

$1/8 + 1/8 + 1/8 + 1/8 + 1/8 = 5/8$

$1/8 + 1/8 + 1/8 + 1/8 + 1/8 + 1/8 + 1/8 = 7/8$

$2/5 + 1/5 = 3/5$ $3/5 + 1/5 = 4/5$

$2/5 + 2/5 = 4/5$ $4/5 + 1/5 = 5/5 = 1$

$3/8 + 3/8 + 1/8 = 7/8$ $7/8 + 1/8 = 8/8 = 1$

Fill in the answers for problems below:

$1/3 + 1/3 =$	$2/4 + 1/4 =$	$3/8 + 3/8 =$
$5/16 + 6/16 =$	$2/5 + 2/5 =$	$7/8 + 1/8 =$
$4/12 + 4/12 =$	$6/12 + 5/12 =$	$3/12 + 4/12 =$
$8/16 + 2/16 =$	$3/16 + 5/16 =$	$9/16 + 5/16 =$
$5/8 + 2/8 =$	$4/8 + 2/8 =$	$3/8 + 2/8 =$
$2/5 + 1/5 =$	$4/5 + 1/5 =$	$3/5 + 1/5 =$
$3/6 + 2/6 =$	$4/6 + 1/6 =$	$2/6 + 2/6 =$

FRACTIONS — ADDING UNIT FRACTIONS, PAGE 265
1 = NUMERATOR   2 = DENOMINATOR   WRITE: 1/2

Add numerators only

$1/3 + 1/3 = 2/3$ $1/4 + 1/4 = 2/4 = 1/2$

$1/4 + 1/4 + 1/4 = 3/4$ $1/8 + 1/8 + 1/8 = 3/8$

$1/5 + 1/5 = 2/5$ $1/5 + 1/5 + 1/5 = 3/5$

$1/5 + 1/5 + 1/5 + 1/5 = 4/5$

$1/8 + 1/8 + 1/8 + 1/8 + 1/8 = 5/8$

$1/8 + 1/8 + 1/8 + 1/8 + 1/8 + 1/8 + 1/8 = 7/8$

$2/5 + 1/5 = 3/5$ $3/5 + 1/5 = 4/5$

$2/5 + 2/5 = 4/5$ $4/5 + 1/5 = 5/5 = 1$

$3/8 + 3/8 + 1/8 = 7/8$ $7/8 + 1/8 = 8/8 = 1$

Fill in the answers for problems below:

$1/3 + 1/3 =$ $2/4 + 1/4 =$ $3/8 + 3/8 =$

$5/16 + 6/16 =$ $2/5 + 2/5 =$ $7/8 + 1/8 =$

$4/12 + 4/12 =$ $6/12 + 5/12 =$ $3/12 + 4/12 =$

$8/16 + 2/16 =$ $3/16 + 5/16 =$ $9/16 + 5/16 =$

$5/8 + 2/8 =$ $4/8 + 2/8 =$ $3/8 + 2/8 =$

$2/5 + 1/5 =$ $4/5 + 1/5 =$ $3/5 + 1/5 =$

$3/6 + 2/6 =$ $4/6 + 1/6 =$ $2/6 + 2/6 =$

FRACTIONS WITH LIKE OR COMMON DENOMINATORS

Fill in the answers for problems below:

$1/3 + 1/3 =$ $2/4 + 1/4 =$ $3/8 + 3/8 =$

$5/16 + 6/16 =$ $2/5 + 2/5 =$ $7/8 + 1/8 =$

$4/12 + 4/12 =$ $6/12 + 5/12 =$ $3/12 + 4/12 =$

$8/16 + 2/16 =$ $3/16 + 5/16 =$ $9/16 + 5/16 =$

$5/8 + 2/8 =$ $4/8 + 2/8 =$ $3/8 + 2/8 =$

$2/5 + 1/5 =$ $4/5 + 1/5 =$ $3/5 + 1/5 =$

$3/6 + 2/6 =$ $4/6 + 1/6 =$ $2/6 + 2/6 =$

$2/7 + 3/7 =$ $1/7 + 5/7 =$ $4/7 + 3/7 =$

$3/9 + 2/9 =$ $4/9 + 2/9 =$ $6/9 + 2/9 =$

$5/10 + 2/10 =$ $4/10 + 4/10 =$ $6/10 + 4/10 =$

$3/11 + 5/11 =$ $6/11 + 3/11 =$ $8/11 + 2/11 =$

$5/12 + 6/12 =$ $9/12 + 3/12 =$ $4/12 + 2/12 =$

FRACTIONS WITH LIKE OR COMMON DENOMINATORS

Fill in the answers for problems below:

1/3 + 1/3 =	2/4 + 1/4 =	3/8 + 3/8 =
5/16 + 6/16 =	2/5 + 2/5 =	7/8 + 1/8 =
4/12 + 4/12 =	6/12 + 5/12 =	3/12 + 4/12 =
8/16 + 2/16 =	3/16 + 5/16 =	9/16 + 5/16 =
5/8 + 2/8 =	4/8 + 2/8 =	3/8 + 2/8 =
2/5 + 1/5 =	4/5 + 1/5 =	3/5 + 1/5 =
3/6 + 2/6 =	4/6 + 1/6 =	2/6 + 2/6 =
2/7 + 3/7 =	1/7 + 5/7 =	4/7 + 3/7 =
3/9 + 2/9 =	4/9 + 2/9 =	6/9 + 2/9 =
5/10 + 2/10 =	4/10 + 4/10 =	6/10 + 4/10 =
3/11 + 5/11 =	6 / 11 + 3 /11 =	8/11 + 2/11 =
5/12 + 6/12 =	9/12 + 3/12 =	4/12 + 2/12 =

FRACTIONS WITH LIKE OR COMMON DENOMINATORS

Fill in the answers for problems below:

1/3 + 1/3 =	2/4 + 1/4 =	3/8 + 3/8 =
5/16 + 6/16 =	2/5 + 2/5 =	7/8 + 1/8 =
4/12 + 4/12 =	6/12 + 5/12 =	3/12 + 4/12 =
8/16 + 2/16 =	3/16 + 5/16 =	9/16 + 5/16 =
5/8 + 2/8 =	4/8 + 2/8 =	3/8 + 2/8 =
2/5 + 1/5 =	4/5 + 1/5 =	3/5 + 1/5 =
3/6 + 2/6 =	4/6 + 1/6 =	2/6 + 2/6 =
2/7 + 3/7 =	1/7 + 5/7 =	4/7 + 3/7 =
3/9 + 2/9 =	4/9 + 2/9 =	6/9 + 2/9 =
5/10 + 2/10 =	4/10 + 4/10 =	6/10 + 4/10 =
3/11 + 5/11 =	6 / 11 + 3 /11 =	8/11 + 2/11 =
5/12 + 6/12 =	9/12 + 3/12 =	4/12 + 2/12 =

REDUCING FRACTIONS — Page 267

Example: $\dfrac{4}{36}$ Divide both numerator and denominator by largest divisor

Think: 4 is a multiple of 36 and 4.

Therefore: $\dfrac{4 \div 4 = 1}{36 \div 4 = 9}$ You now have the lowest term

When a fraction cannot be divided evenly anymore, you have reduced it to its lowest term.

Reduce the fractions below to their lowest terms.

4/10 =	5/20 =	8/12 =	14/24 =
4/24 =	12/16 =	4/6 =	2/24 =
10/20 =	6/8 =	8/24 =	4/12 =
4/16 =	3/6 =	8/16 =	10/24 =
2/12 =	4/8 =	14/16 =	18/24 =
16/24 =	9/24 =	6/20 =	4/20 =
12/24 =	16/20 =	6/24 =	2/16 =
8/20 =	14/20 =	10/12 =	15/20 =
4/16 =	10/16 =	6/10 =	5/10 =

REDUCING FRACTIONS — Page 267

Example: 4   Divide both numerator and
                36 denominator by largest divisor
Think: 4 is a multiple of 36 and 4.
Therefore: 4 ÷ 4 = 1
              36 ÷ 4 = 9 You now have the lowest term

When a fraction cannot be divided evenly anymore,
you have reduced it to its lowest term.

Reduce the fractions below to their lowest terms.

4/10 =	5/20 =	8/12 =	14/24 =
4/24 =	12/16 =	4/6 =	2/24 =
10/20 =	6/8 =	8/24 =	4/12 =
4/16 =	3/6 =	8/16 =	10/24 =
2/12 =	4/8 =	14/16 =	18/24 =
16/24 =	9/24 =	6/20 =	4/20 =
12/24 =	16/20 =	6/24 =	2/16 =
8/20 =	14/20 =	10/12 =	15/20 =
4/16 =	10/16 =	6/10 =	5/10 =

REDUCING FRACTIONS — Page 267

Example: $\underline{4}$ Divide both numerator and
         36 denominator by largest divisor
Think: 4 is a multiple of 36 and 4.
Therefore: 4 ÷ 4 = 1
           36 ÷ 4 = 9 You now have the lowest term

When a fraction cannot be divided evenly anymore, you have reduced it to its lowest term.

Reduce the fractions below to their lowest terms.

4/10 =	5/20 =	8/12 =	14/24 =
4/24 =	12/16 =	4/6 =	2/24 =
10/20 =	6/8 =	8/24 =	4/12 =
4/16 =	3/6 =	8/16 =	10/24 =
2/12 =	4/8 =	14/16 =	18/24 =
16/24 =	9/24 =	6/20 =	4/20 =
12/24 =	16/20 =	6/24 =	2/16 =
8/20 =	14/20 =	10/12 =	15/20 =
4/16 =	10/16 =	6/10 =	5/10 =

REDUCING FRACTIONS — MORE PRACTICE
Page 268
Use the largest number that you can see will divide both the numerator and denominator.

6/15 =	15/48 =	30/48 =	12/15 =
12/30 =	9/48 =	8/64 =	6/48 =
24/32 =	3/18 =	14/64 =	5/30 =
10/25 =	3/9 =	4/18 =	20/32 =
16/48 =	15/18 =	6/9 =	42/48 =
4/14 =	12/18 =	21/30 =	24/64 =
9/15 =	20/25 =	10/18 =	10/15 =
36/64 =	2/14 =	5/25 =	48/64 =
16/32 =	12/32 =	12/14 =	26/30 =
30/32 =	56/64 =	15/25 =	24/30 =
28/32 =	10/14 =	6/18 =	24/48 =
20/64 =	5/15 =	6/14 =	10/30 =

REDUCING FRACTIONS — MORE PRACTICE
Page 268
Use the largest number that you can see will divide
both the numerator and denominator.

6/15 =   15/48 =   30/48 =   12/15 =

12/30 =   9/48 =   8/64 =   6/48 =

24/32 =   3/18 =   14/64 =   5/30 =

10/25 =   3/9 =   4/18 =   20/32 =

16/48 =   15/18 =   6/9 =   42/48 =

4/14 =   12/18 =   21/30 =   24/64 =

9/15 =   20/25 =   10/18 =   10/15 =

36/64 =   2/14 =   5/25 =   48/64 =

16/32 =   12/32 =   12/14 =   26/30 =

30/32 =   56/64 =   15/25 =   24/30 =

28/32 =   10/14 =   6/18 =   24/48 =

20/64 =   5/15 =   6/14 =   10/30 =

REDUCING FRACTIONS — MORE PRACTICE
Page 268
Use the largest number that you can see will divide both the numerator and denominator.

6/15 =	15/48 =	30/48 =	12/15 =
12/30 =	9/48 =	8/64 =	6/48 =
24/32 =	3/18 =	14/64 =	5/30 =
10/25 =	3/9 =	4/18 =	20/32 =
16/48 =	15/18 =	6/9 =	42/48 =
4/14 =	12/18 =	21/30 =	24/64 =
9/15 =	20/25 =	10/18 =	10/15 =
36/64 =	2/14 =	5/25 =	48/64 =
16/32 =	12/32 =	12/14 =	26/30 =
30/32 =	56/64 =	15/25 =	24/30 =
28/32 =	10/14 =	6/18 =	24/48 =
20/64 =	5/15 =	6/14 =	10/30 =

ANSWERS TO PROBLEMS, COMMON DENOMINATORS:

ROW 1: 2/3, 3/4, 6/8
ROW 2: 11/16, 4/5, 8/8 or 1
ROW 3: 8/12, 11/12, 7/12
ROW 4: 10/16, 8/16, 14/16
ROW 5: 7/8, 6/8, 5/8
ROW 6: 3/5, 5/5 or 1, 4/5
ROW 7: 5/6, 5/6, 4/6
ROW 8: 5/7, 6/7, 7/7 or 1
ROW 9: 5/9, 6/9, 8/9
ROW 10: 7/10, 8/10, 10/10 or 1
ROW 11: 8/11, 9/11, 10/11
ROW 12: 11/12, 12/12 or 1, 6/12

ANSWERS FOR PAGE 267:

ROW 1: 2/5, 1/4, 2/3, 7/12
ROW 2: 1/6, 3/4, 2/3, 1/12
ROW 3: 1/2, 3/4, 1/3, 1/3
ROW 4: 1/4, 1/2, 1/2, 5/12
ROW 5: 1/6, 1/2, 7/8, 3/4
ROW 6: 2/3, 3/8, 3/10, 1/5
ROW 7: 1/2, 4/5, 1/4, 1/8
ROW 8: 2/5, 7/10, 5/6, 3/4
ROW 9: 1/4, 5/8, 3/5, 1/2

ANSWERS PAGE 268:

ROW 1: 2/5, 5/16, 5/8, 4/5
ROW 2: 2/5, 3/16, 1/8, 1/8
ROW 3: 3/4, 1/6, 7/32, 1/6
ROW 4: 2/5, 1/3, 2/9, 5/8
ROW 5: 1/3, 5/6, 2/3, 7/8
ROW 6: 2/7, 2/3, 7/10, 3/8
ROW 7: 3/5, 4/5, 5/9, 2/3
ROW 8: 9/16. 1/7. 1/5. 3/4

ROW 9: 1/2, 3/8, 6/7, 13/15
ROW 10: 15/16, 7/8, 3/5, 4/5
ROW 11: 7/8, 5/7, 1/3, 1/2
ROW 12: 5/16, 1/3, 3/7, 1/3

www.ingramcontent.com/pod-product-compliance
Lightning Source LLC
Chambersburg PA
CBHW082012290326
41934CB00014BA/3285